THE COLORS OF PORTLAND

THE COLORS OF PORTLAND

VICTORIA KENT

Inscribe Press
Creativity Unleashed

Hillsboro, OR

Published by Inscribe Press, Hillsboro, OR
Cover design and interior art by Abbey Chaplain (https://studiogail.co)

Printed in the United States of America.

ISBN 978-1-951611-39-2 (print)

DEDICATION

This book is dedicated to my family who inspired me to dream big and soar, supported my trip to the west coast in so many ways, and trusted the Lord as they let their baby girl leave the nest at twenty years old to move out west.

My Mom – Vanessa

My Dad – David

My Brother – Christian

My Sister – Ashlyn

CONTENTS

INTRODUCTION

I will never forget the day Victoria Kent emerged into our world. It happened in form of an email. I had just arrived at the Father's House offices and opened my email. One email caught my eye because of the subject title, "looking for internship with church in Portland." That caught my eye, because we just started an internship program but had not advertised it. I read the email and there was such sincerity and purity in the inquiry that I forwarded it to our internship director and said, "check this email out and let's get this girl into our internship." That fall. Victoria packed up everything and moved to Portland, where she fully engaged in our mission to love the city and reach it for the Kingdom. To engage its most difficult issues with a heart of a servant and the wisdom that comes from above.

The Colors of Portland is about Victoria's discovery of God's heart towards our city. Cities are a big deal to God; look how He talks about Jerusalem throughout the scriptures with such love and good will. He sent Jonah to save Nineveh because He loved Nineveh. Cities are such a big deal to Him that He ends the temporal history of man on Earth by bringing a city down from Heaven that He calls His dwelling place, where He will dwell with men (Revelation 21:1-3). In this book you will see how Victoria starts to look at the city not how it presently is, but how God wants it to be. In the midst of a season of riots, wildfires, and unrest, she catches what Portland is called to be and joins us in the fight to bring that about. This book will inspire what is possible: that city transformation can happen. That we belong to an ever-advancing Kingdom and when we catch the Kingdom intent for a city and its people, nothing is impossible. Especially when we rise in courage.

Victoria's courage is not really highlighted in the stories you will read as it should be — due to her humility — but let me highlight it. God impressed me to have a team that would go where the 2020 riots were occurring to pray and bring peace. Victoria was one of only a few women who volunteered; it was mostly men who stepped up because it was like a call to war.

But Victoria did what even the men didn't do. She went right to the front lines of the demonstration where a fence divided the protesters from the police and the police station. The protesters were yelling the most hateful words and curses at the police, but I saw Victoria step right up on the fence, and she began yelling also, but with shouts of, "we love you; we are praying for you!" She motioned to an officer to come over to her, and then proceeded to pour out God's love on this officer who had been maligned, and hit with frozen bottles of water and bricks. She did it right there next to the people who had thrown those bottles and bricks. And God protected her. She was able to do this because she had learned her identity as God's daughter. She had learned that our fight is with unseen forces and how we are to engage with those forces. She had discovered how to discern the voice of God in the midst of chaos. All things you will learn about in this book.

I testify that the stories are true and that the principles she shares in this book are responsible for the revival that Portland is now coming into. All because there are a people who refuse to look at a city through eyes of the flesh, but instead see it with the true colors that God designed it to carry.

Steve Trujillo
Senior leader and founding pastor, Father's House City Ministries

THE LAND OF ENTREPRENEURS & COFFEE

Just as an artist adds layers of paint on a canvas until the designs begin to take shape, the colors over the city of Portland blend into a brilliant panorama, representing a greater story that points to a heavenly blueprint. The colors on the canvas represent the power of creativity flowing from heaven into human hands. These colors of creativity manifest through art, imagination, ideas, strategies, and dreams coming to fruition, covering all areas of society, culture, and influence. This kind of creativity enables the artists to solve complex problems in society. Over time, these colors, subtly illuminate the canvas. As the canvas is filled with colors, the culture of Portland is filled with heavens blueprint with strategic assignments the leaders, entrepreneurs, and creatives in the city carry. As you look closer, you can see that each color is a crucial part for the greater story, and they bring light and glory when the canvas is finally finished. Portland, known as "the city of roses," blooms where there had been thorns. Where darkness currently rests over the city, the truth, the glory of God, and the colors of heaven pierce through it all.

As a newcomer, I fell in love with the dreamy Pacific Northwest culture. Friends and family have repeatedly commented, "Victoria, you wear Portland and fit so well in the culture." "I thought you were raised here in Portland!"

People are often surprised to find that I'm originally an east coast native. Growing up I had never been west of Tennessee. But in January 2018, at twenty years old and in the middle of my foundational college years, I made a radical decision to sell my belongings and move to Portland, Oregon serve as an intern with a church ministry. I left my family, friends, and car out east, and missed my chance of ever getting that "ring before spring" at my college university. Looking back, I wonder how I survived the first eight months in Portland without a car, a paid job, and not much money in my bank account. But amid uncertainty, God's hand rested over my life and led the way. God divinely set in place a spiritual family waiting for me to arrive on the west coast.

Portland is where my heart is. If you have never been to Portland, let me tell you a bit about this vibrant and quirky city. It has a small town feel with the depth, culture, and movement of a big city. The moment you enter downtown, you will see a multitude of trees surrounding the city streets. Twelve unique bridges over the city give locals and visitors fantastic views as they walk, bike, run, or drive throughout the city limits.

Portland is known for its hiking trails just outside the city limits. And not too far away is the majestic Mt. Hood. If it's a clear day, you will see Mt. Hood in the distance standing tall with snow on it all year long. Portland is centrally located to a ski lodge, and volcanoes, and just a couple of hours away is the glorious, rocky Pacific coastline. The city contains a variety of tourist attractions as it is known for its food (it is a renowned "foodie city), organic culture, progressivism, highly skilled baristas, and business makers and creatives.

When you enter the culture of Portland, you will see art plastered everywhere: on buildings, in the architecture, in the clothes, and the artist designs are even incorporated in the coffee latte art. Portland, Oregon sign in the middle of Old Town lights up with a stag on it that can be seen from the west side of the burnside bridge. Portland is the land of entrepreneurs, art, coffee, and weird vibes. I felt at home the moment I stepped off the plane in September 2018.

Upon arrival, I immediately noticed a couple of things in Portland that I don't normally find in other cities:

- One of the city's slogans is "Keep Portland weird."
- Vegan/vegetarian friendly
- The coffee is beyond excellent! Get ready to pay for $6 to $7 lattes
- You don't pump your own gas. (It is actually illegal to do so)
- Cannabis shops are on just about every corner and they now deliver to your door.
- It rains a lot here, but it usually sprinkles in a diagonal direction
- No sales tax! (God bless)
- Homeless tents are on every corner (The homeless vacation here)

- The bicyclists know what they're doing more than the drivers
- Feminism headquarters
- Halloween headquarters all year round
- Vitamin d3 supplements are a must because seasonal depression is real

Tragically, beneath the creative vibes lies Portland's darker history of indigenous mistreatment, immigrant exploitation, and human trafficking. Today there remains a darkness covering the city manifested in an overwhelming homeless population, drug abuse, racial unrest, violence, and spiritual brokenness. Yet, I wrote this book to communicate a heavenly perspective of God's vision and heart for this city. I'm so thrilled to share with you how I was directed to Portland and to describe my journey of overcoming fear, demonic spirits in the atmosphere, and my journey of partnering with a spiritual community who strategically walk in power and authority with the agenda of bringing heaven to earth.

You will read about my continuous journey, how I exercised the "Word" of God in the day and the spiritual gifts that were inside of me all along. You will hear about how I:

- Combatted and "wrestled" with the forces of darkness—Living out Ephesians 6 on the front lines
- Grew in discernment, prophecy, and hearing the voice of God
- Broke off past negatives agreements and received layers of deep healing
- Learned how to strategically dismantle demonic spirits and call ideologies out of atmospheres, neighborhoods, cities, and mountains of influence
- Rooted myself in a strong church community with spiritual mothers and fathers
- Worshiped and praised my way through moments of feeling like I was going to be taken out
- Exercised and tapped into the creativity God has given me by using it to advance His Kingdom and manifest heaven's blueprints to earth in Portland as it is in heaven.

This is a continual, accelerated cycle of practical and spiritual growth. I have not yet arrived, so even though it is written in the past tense, I'm continuing to go from glory to glory!

I asked people located in the Portland area what heaven has to say about the city. Heaven says Portland is:

- A city full of color;
- A hotspot for revival, worship, and discipleship;
- Where the presence of God rests and the glory of God is spread throughout the city;
- A Righteous City;
- A place of restoration and full of people who belong;
- A land where innovation and creativity thrive;
- A place where fatherlessness is being redeemed;
- A location that where there is injustice, the sovereignty and goodness of God reigns;
- Where people will be set free and delivered;
- Where followers of Jesus will confront the darkness, stand on the front lines, and call forth the truth of Isaiah 60 over the land;
- A place of unity between the churches;
- Where pastors, evangelists, teachers, prophets, and apostles will rise up out of the normal, safe Christian lifestyle and begin to stand in the gap for our city;
- A place where the sleepers will wake up, rise up, and believe they are sons and daughters of the living God.

Throughout this book you will read about fourteen spiritual and practical keys I walked through in my journey of living in the Pacific Northwest. The keys touch on the topics of spiritual warfare, rest, hearing God's voice, creativity, discovering my spiritual community, and growing in wisdom and discernment. These lessons are practical to all followers of Jesus that can be applied in all cities and mountains of influence.

Key #1: God may speak in unique and unusual ways.

Open your eyes and ears to multiple ways for God to move and speak. He led me to Portland in the strangest way: through the power of Google and email. But here I am, thriving in the beautiful city of Portland that just needs a reminder of who she is. I could not have made this happen. God divinely connected me to a church that has sowed into the land for twenty years prior to me moving here.

Get ready to be blown away by the purpose and destiny of this colorful and vibrant city. Heavenly creativity oozes from Portland, and I have the privilege of living here and witnessing the colors that were once dark resurrect into beautiful light. I hope you will be able to see Portland through heaven's lenses. All eyes have been watching Portland. News networks carry opinions of Portland. You probably have even heard rumors about what has been going on here. Some things you may have heard might be true; but have you heard the rumor that revival birthed out of Portland during the 1904 Welsh revival? The deep wells of revival are ready to burst forth. The land of Portland is crying out for the glory of God to be revealed!

"Then my favor will bathe you in sunlight until you are like the dawn bursting through a dark night. And then suddenly your healing will manifest. You will see your righteousness march out before you, and the glory of Yahweh will protect you from all harm!" Isaiah 58:8, TPT

This book is an invitation to see Portland through the eyes of heaven and agree that God's glory is greater than the darkness in the "Nineveh" cities. God intends for you to walk in the fullness of your destiny. He intends that you have, life, and life abundantly; living in fullness so that you can awaken sons and daughters to the truth of Jesus and align earth to the realities of heaven wherever you are. This means walking in the spiritual authority that you have been given. "Truly, I say to you, whatever you bind on earth shall be bound in heaven, and whatever you loose on earth shall be loosed in heaven. Again, I say to you, if two of you agree on earth about anything they ask, it will be done for them by my Father in heaven. For where two or three are gathered in my name, there am I among them." Matthew 18:18-20, NIV

My heart is for you to tap into the fullness of your authority in Christ and to confidently walk into becoming the man or woman God designed you to be! You were made to transform culture; to bring heaven to earth. There are so many intricate gifts God placed inside of you that might not have been released yet or even revealed to you.

On the next page, I have some questions for you.

1. How does God speak to you? Are you open to hearing him in multiple ways?
2. How do you battle spiritual warfare when you are feeling attacked emotionally or physically? How do you wear your armor? (Talked about in Ephesians 6)
3. What Mountain(s) of influence has God called you to? Media, Business/ Economy, Arts + entertainment, Family, Religion, Government, and Education.
4. Do you partner with the Holy Spirit to bring His presence, love, and glory into your city, neighborhood, house, or workplace? What does that look like for you to invite the presence of God into these spaces?
5. Do you have a grounded spiritual community who supports you, even corrects you at times, but most importantly cover you in prayer when you need it most?
6. Do you believe you are creative and if so, what does it look like to invite the Holy Spirit into that creative space? Keep these questions in the forefront of your mind as we journey through *The Colors of Portland* together.

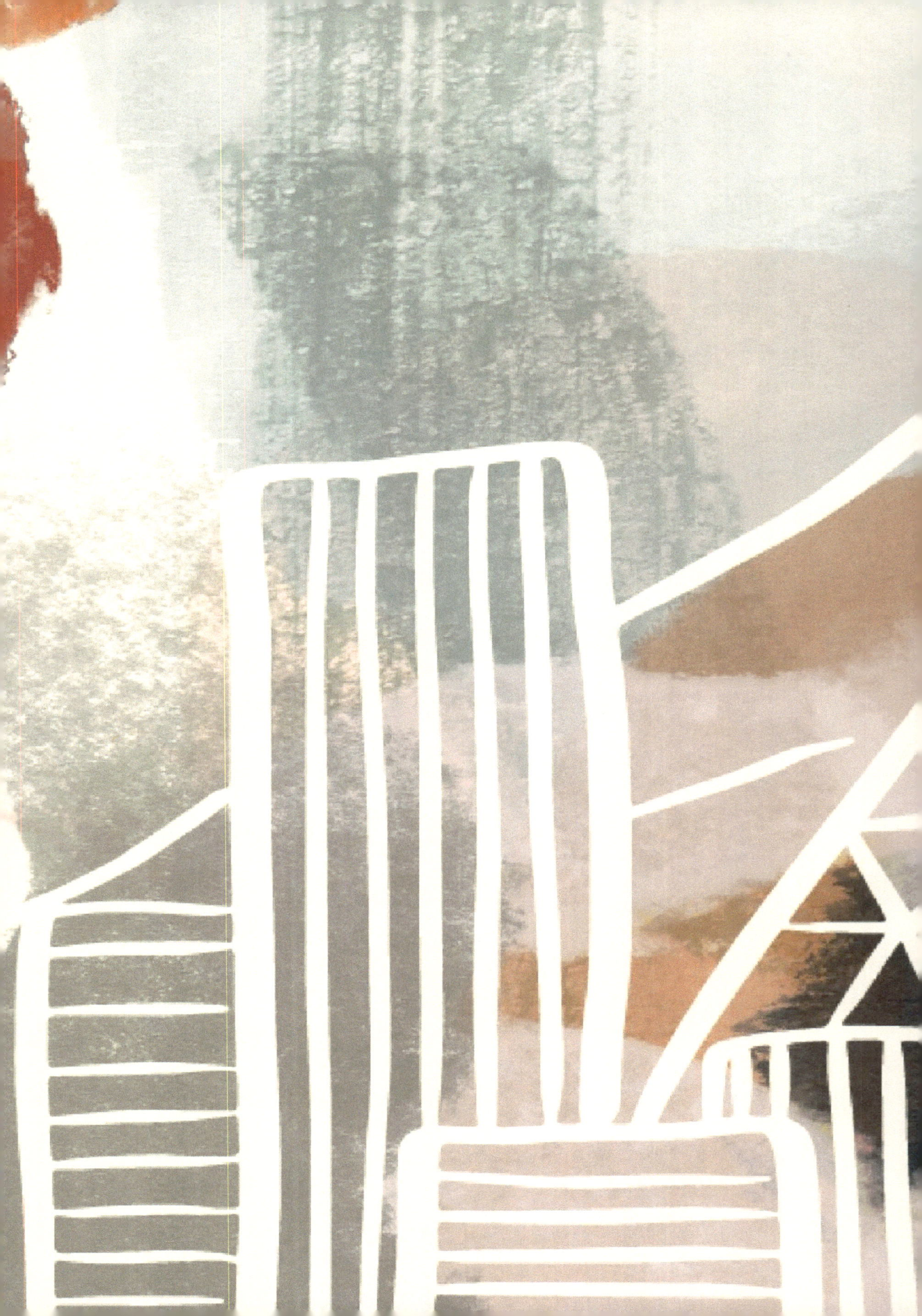

VIRGINIA TO PORTLAND

In January 2018, I lived in Virginia Beach enjoying my junior year of college, involved in intramural basketball and volleyball, and surrounded by a solid spirit-filled community. I felt extremely plugged in and was thriving at a church called Big House Church. These were my foundational years of being filled with the spirit, learning how to walk in evangelism, and in my spiritual gifts. I had called myself a Christian all my life but never walked in the supernatural until my freshman year of college.

I probably would not have been given the opportunity to move to Portland if God had not set up my college experience to create a strong spiritual foundation as a launching pad to greater things. In my first few years of college, I witnessed God's hand as He surrounded me with a spirit-filled community on campus and a church community that supported my spiritual journey , which gave me direction to grow in hearing God's voice. This opened the door to move to Portland.

At the end of high school, before entering the college world, I had not experienced being filled with the Spirit. I struggled hearing God's voice and lacked confidence that He spoke to me. During the end of my senior year of high school, my dad helped me apply to ten to fifteen universities. I desired to attend a well-known school in the Appalachian Mountains where a large percentage of my high school friends planned on attending. To encourage me even more, my boyfriend at the time, was already attending there, and on top of that I had a roommate situation set up. A couple months closer to the school deadline, I lost my roommate and my boyfriend. The doors closed to attend that school. I was disappointed, because I had put all my eggs in one basket and saw my future in the Appalachian Mountains. I was drawn to the earthy and hipster atmosphere in the mountains. However, I would have probably been swept away by the heavy atmosphere of depression and witchcraft there. God protected me from attending that school because I was not spiritually prepared to be in that setting without a solid spiritual community.

A couple weeks later after dealing with my two disappointments, my dad offered to drive me three hours away to tour Regent University in Virginia Beach. I hesitated, because I was not interested in going, but then agreed. After a long three-hour drive, I stepped on campus and even though I was still a bit closed off to attending Regent, my ears perked up as I glanced at the campus. The tour guide was very friendly, and I clearly remember noticing specific words that stuck out to me. "Regent's mission is Christian Leadership to Change the World." Those words resonated in my spirit and for what seemed like the first time, I could feel the Holy Spirit moving powerfully on the campus. My heart softened and I felt more open to receive. I could sense the glory and the presence of God. As I walked through the halls, the chapel, and other buildings during the tour, I could feel the weight of the years of prayer, vision, and worship released over the campus.

At the end of the tour, I looked at my dad and said, "I'm ready to sign the papers to attend here." I ended up applying just before the deadline.

Regent's rich spiritual history stemmed from Pat Robertson's vision in 1977. Pat envisioned having a seventy -acre land with a university that trains and equips women and men into leaders, with the vision of changing the world with quality education and solid biblical teaching.[1] That fall, I started classes and moved to Virginia Beach, Virginia. A pool of students from a variety of denominations attended there. I began to experience the Holy Spirit on a new level I had not experienced before. The first week of school I immediately started searching for the right church. I found quite a few non-denominational churches that felt similar to churches back in North Carolina. However, everything changed after I experienced a healing encounter when I was dealing with a cold and low blood sugar one evening.

Towards the end of my senior year of high school, I dealt with a leaky gut and low blood sugar that quickly forced me to change my eating habits by eating snacks every couple of hours. I got used to bringing snacks everywhere as a student on campus. During the time I was church hopping, I found a church that met Saturday evenings. Towards the end of the service, I started getting dizzy and realized I needed my snack. On top of that, I had a sore throat and was dealing with cold symptoms. At the end of the service, the pastor called out for anyone

1 https://www.regent.edu/about-regent/

who needed healing in their body to receive prayer at the front. In that moment, I felt an obvious tug from the Holy Spirit to go forward and ask for prayer. It took some boldness to walk up there. This kind of tug on my heart was new to me, but it was so clear that God was speaking to me in a gentle way. I hesitated at first, but the thought didn't go away. I knew I would regret it if I didn't at least ask for prayer.

The lady who prayed over me said a very simple prayer after I shared about my cold and my blood sugar issues. I told her that I just wanted to feel normal again and be healed from my gut problems. As she said this simple prayer, I began feeling heat and tingling all over my body. Suddenly, I saw a dark cloud that started in my gut slowly leave my body. I had never seen anything like that before. After the prayer, my body felt lighter, and energy began to invigorate me. I wanted to run around and dance as I was not feeling dizzy after that. Interestingly, I still had a sore throat, but my other symptoms changed. I encountered the supernatural healing power of Jesus in that moment. This was a fresh encounter and touch from the Holy Spirit. It was as if a veil had been removed, leading me into a deeper understanding of who Jesus is as my healer. I read stories in the Bible about Jesus healing, and I prayed for people to feel better from sickness or cancer, thinking that in time they would be healed, but I'm not sure if I ever believed that God could heal in an instant. My opinion changed after that powerful encounter.

I was only a couple of months into college, and that experience changed my direction and perspective forever! God holds the power to heal. From that point on, that encounter was a turning point for my spiritual journey. I found myself surrounded by a community that encouraged people and pointed them to Christ. As I attended weekly university chapel nights, stepping into worship gave me freedom and a deeper revelation of Jesus and my identity in him, and I began to tap into the authority revealed in the Bible that we as followers of Jesus are given. Matthew 10:7-8 "*As you go, proclaim this message: 'The kingdom of heaven has come near.' Heal the sick, raise the dead, cleanse those who have leprosy, drive out demons. Freely you have* received; freely give."

I eventually found my church home in Virginia Beach. One Sunday afternoon, a group of ten of us from school attended this church called Big House. I was intrigued by the name. It was in the heart of downtown Ghent, VA. The area was quite beautiful and different than Virginia Beach, as it was located in an area with streets of cobblestone, aesthetic coffee shops nearby, and cute 100-year-old cottage-like houses. The church was in an old Methodist building with beautiful stained-glass windows and wooden pews. The main service started at 4:00 p.m., and it was stunning to watch the sun peek through the windows during worship.

The ground would shake as we got rowdy in worship, with lots of freedom, dancing, and people twirling flags. I noticed that many of the people who attended wore fedora hats; the men sported beards and man buns, and the women wore thrifted clothes. It was a vibe. The pre-service prayer really surprised me as I heard loud singing and speaking in tongues leading up to the service in the other room. I was really attracted to this kind of atmosphere even though it felt unfamiliar. A few visits later, I called Big House home! Soon after, I plugged into evangelism teams, and quickly connected with the pastors, leaders, and those who attended the church. Everywhere I would go, my desire to share the gospel exploded. I found myself evangelizing to strangers daily, sharing the gospel, praying for those in pain, and giving words of knowledge. I carried supernatural boldness that I had never seen in me before.

Throughout the months, friends from my university asked if I had received my spiritual language. I was interested in receiving it but didn't understand how it worked. I thought maybe the Holy Spirit possessed people who received tongues and I would not be able to control it. At first, I felt a bit weird being in places where people would start speaking in tongues when I was not able to yet. I thought maybe God would take control over my voice and it would flow that way. I found myself frustrated that I hadn't received a spiritual language after prayer from those who flowed in it. One evening in my room, it was just me and the Lord, and as I prayed a couple of words came out that I had never said out loud. It took me time to realize that God wanted to partner with me, rather than Him taking over and possessing my tongue. I later realized that speaking in tongues was more a muscle to practice, and tap into, requiring me to humble myself and allow the Holy Spirit to move through me.

CHANGE IN SEASONS

I spent a year and a half at the Regent campus, and then God began to speak to me about direction and future plans. I was set up to graduate in three years rather than four. That meant my summer study load consisted of fifteenth to eighteen hours of credits. One semester I even took twenty-one hours. With graduation not too far off, I began to think about the required internships in my senior year.

As I was in the middle of a season of growing in hearing God's voice, there was a testing moment in my life where I believed I heard God's voice. In, January 2018 my church congregation pursued the Daniel Fast for twenty-one days. During that time, I sought direction from God for the upcoming year, and at the end of the fast, I heard the voice of God.

I remember the exact moment. I sat at my desk in my dorm room working on homework. I heard a soft voice in my head saying, "Look up spirit-filled churches in Portland, Oregon for your internship." I thought to myself, "Where did that thought come from? I have never been to Portland, nor do I know anything about that state."

Even though I did not understand where the thought came from, a few minutes later I decided to look up "spirit-filled churches in Portland." I had searched for an internship to finish my bachelor's degree during that semester, but assumed I would intern somewhere in Virginia nearby my school. My degree was in Communications and Journalism, but I felt directed by the Lord to be involved in a ministry-focused internship. After a few minutes of researching, "Father's House City Ministries" showed up as one of the top searches in Google. I had poked around other internships but had not heard back from anyone, so I decided it wouldn't hurt to send another email. I mustered up the courage to send a spontaneous email to the pastor.

Hi Steve,

My name is Victoria Kent. I am currently in school at Regent University near Virginia Beach and have been looking for an internship at a church in the west. I am graduating in about a year and would love to be a missionary over in Europe for the long-term goal after past travel experiences there. But in this season, I believe the Holy Spirit has been directing me to Portland, Oregon.

You are probably wondering why out west? I am not a 100% sure but for a while now my heart has been desiring to go to Portland, Oregon. I was looking online for spirit-filled churches in Portland, and I felt drawn to the Fathers House. So, this is just where I am at.

I love being a part of ministry and love working with all ages but also specifically have been involved with a little bit of writing, preaching, evangelism, worship, and ministry with kids and young adults.

Let me know if you guys would like an intern with any of those areas. I truly just want to serve. I know this email is very much out of the blue, but I just felt like I needed to obey the Lord and see where he is directing me in this moment.

Blessings,
Victoria

Just a few days later, I received an email back.

Hi Victoria,

Thank you for reaching out to us. God is putting Portland in lots of people because of what He is doing here in bringing revival and that unlocks reformation that releasing lasting cultural transformation. So, it doesn't surprise us that you are being drawn here, God is up to something great. Also, Portland is called to be a great Port to export the Kingdom all around the world. It will be a great place to be launched into foreign ministry work.

I would like to introduce you to our executive pastor who oversees our internship ministry. It would be great for you guys to connect and discern what the Lord maybe doing.

Blessings,
Steve

That weekend after sending the email, I attended Big House and I clearly remember the pastor during the transition time after worship saying, "Big House is looking a lot like Father's House!" My jaw dropped and I knew the Lord was speaking to me through those words even though the pastor was speaking in the context of heaven. My heart was flooded with peace and excitement and I felt like I was exploding inside, even though the whole situation did not make sense. Looking back, this experience seemed a little spiritual and insane, but God was clearly in the middle of it.

I remember going to one of my favorite thrift stores in North Carolina a few weeks later. As I looked through the clothes, a shirt caught my attention, because the front was boldly printed, "Portland, Oregon." When I looked closer, I was shocked to find the shirt behind it on the rack read "Victoria."

I still have a photo of the shirts on my phone that shows the silliest ways God speaks to me. A Portland, Oregon shirt in North Carolina?! You can't make this kind of stuff up!

So, in January 2018, I heard the voice of God directing me to Portland and by September 2018, I moved to Portland and stayed with the executive pastors of the church. The quiet words I heard from the Lord "*look up spirit filled churches*" birthed a reality eight months later. I spent the following eight months serving under Father's House City Ministries.

Little did I know that the church God aligned me with in Portland had been sowing and pouring into the city for over twenty years, with leaders who had knowledge of the history of buildings and underground secrets of the land.

Before Father's House pioneered the longest-standing congregation in downtown Portland, every church downtown would die within two years. The downtown area was known as the "graveyard of churches." No one could put their finger on it, but churches would shut down or move to a different location outside of the main downtown area within two years or less of locating there. Many assume the heavy amount of witchcraft that occurred in the downtown area moved congregations out. The homeless issue could have also been a main component as well. The downtown area of Portland seemed to control the entire political state of Oregon even though it is not the capital. However, Father's House was the first ministry that did not come under the intimidation of being planted downtown. Isaiah 60 embodies the call and assignment of Father's House.

Isaiah 60 starts out with "Arise, Jerusalem, let your light shine for all to see. For the Glory of the Lord rises to shine on you. Darkness as black as night covers all the nations of the earth, but the glory of the Lord rises and appears over you…"(NLT)

Amid darkness in Portland, the glory of the Lord shines greater over the city. This is a promise I will always hold.

Years before I moved to Portland, Father's House spent two decades sowing into the Portland State University campus, in the area where churches would eventually die off within two years of being planted. There was a time during a move of God on campus where the entire football team got saved. But gradually, the hunger for God on campus dissipated. The students seemed uninterested in spiritual things.

Pastor Steve remembered a time where students would wander into his church office on campus and confess the depression and heaviness they were feeling living on campus. Students on campus experienced huge depression and isolation and felt there was no one at school they could connect with. But there came a block in the spirit, to the point that evangelism teams would minister on campus, and people were not interested in knowing the God who healed them.

The prayer team from Fathers House received a strategy to prayer walk and map out the land in a specific area on campus. The group eventually discovered altars to other gods that pointed to the spiritual blockage of mass salvations. Many may think that altars are a thing of the past and are only mentioned in the Old Testament where certain cultures made sacrifices to other gods. However, witchcraft and occult practices are quite popular in Portland and sacrifices are still made to other gods. A few days after the team worshipped and prayed for the altars to be removed, there was immediate change the following week in how people received the gospel during evangelism outreach. Soon after that, five people got saved on campus, and it was the beginning signs of revival at Portland State University.

SPIRITUAL MAPPING + HISTORY OF PORTLAND

There is something powerful about studying the history of the founders and the covenants that were made in certain lands. It gives insight to why the forces of darkness have authority in certain places, and why they want that authority. Where the enemy may try to show himself at work over lands, there is often a greater intent behind it. We as followers of Jesus reverse the trend by releasing the kingdom values over the land. Heaven and hell both need the agreement of men. If we don't agree with Heaven, our silence will give hell a foothold. There is a battle between good and evil and often it shows up in territory and land. Have you ever experienced crossing over a boundary line in a state and feeling completely different a few minutes later? Or walking into a business and just feeling icky the whole time you are in the store? Maybe you cross over a bridge and feel heaviness or hear thoughts that have never come to your mind before. There is something powerful about land and partnership with the authority owning land. Matthew 18:18-20 talks about whatever we bind, loose, and declare on earth shall be bound in heaven. God has given humans authority over the natural but also spiritually. We have the authority to prophesy, heal the sick, cast out demons, raise the dead, and bring heaven to earth in culture and areas of influence. We also have authority over spaces and places where agreements have been made. Land holds memory and manifests as either righteous or evil and affects the culture today even if there was an event that occurred hundreds of years before.

Spiritual mapping is a practical way to understand the natural and spiritual history of an area, leading to practical and spiritual knowledge that opens the door to prayer points that reveal strategy for removing evil and replacing it with righteousness in the land. I learned about this kind of mapping from Pastor Steve and the city transformation outreach teams. My experience walking the streets of Portland changed my perspective forever on how to take authority over lands and atmospheres.

While prayer walking or mapping, more than likely there will be things discovered that need to be uprooted as you walk about. However, transformation over cities is a process. This process may look like mapping the land, prayer walking, taking care of those in need, building, and serving. Serve the city in which you live. You might not know where to serve until you map. Serve and build at these broken places. Serving releases favor to bring heaven to earth in areas of influence, allows the light of God to infiltrate people and places, and restores broken places. Isaiah 60 talks about how the glory of God rises in the midst of darkness but Isaiah 58 is our responsibility, giving the action steps for the glory to come. Heaven is waiting for us to partner with rebuilding the ruins. Rebuilding looks like serving in the local community outside of the four walls, prayer walking with a team, worshiping over these areas, taking care of the homeless, infiltrating the mountains of influence with kingdom strategy (government, education.etc..), and serving where there is a need.

Isaiah 58: 6-9, NIV *"Is not this the kind of fasting I have chosen: to loose the chains of injustice and untie the cords of the yoke, to set the oppressed free and break every yoke? 7 Is it not to share your food with the hungry and to provide the poor wanderer with shelter— when you see the naked, to clothe them, and not to turn away from your own flesh and blood? 8 Then your light will break forth like the dawn, and your healing will quickly appear; then your righteousness will go before you, and the glory of the Lord will be your rear guard. 9 Then you will call, and the Lord will answer; you will cry for help, and he will say: Here am I."*

Verse 8 explains what will come after *"loosing the chains of injustice, setting the oppressed free, sharing food with the hungry, and clothing the naked"*: *"Then your light will break forth like the dawn, and your healing will quickly appear; then your righteousness will go before you, and the glory of the Lord will be your rear guard."*

The glory comes after the rebuilding and serving. God desires for the righteous to occupy territory to extend this Kingdom and bring it into its destiny. Don't sleep on spiritual mapping. It's an important key to bringing transformation. When looking into spiritual mapping, the first thing to do is research, going back as far back there is data, to understand partnerships between evil and righteousness. When mapping, it is essential to partner with the Holy Spirit and ask for His heart for the destiny of the specific area. Mapping, prayer, and worship all go hand-in hand, for from his presence flows fruit, breakthrough, and transformation. When Father's House first discovered the historical roots of Portland, they began to understand the reasons churches died after two years in the downtown area. The leadership team of Father's House began to map out the land of Portland. They intentionally looked for answers about the missionaries who came to the area and the existing trends of over the land, and what agreements were made when the area was first inhabited. Trends established by the individuals who first inhabited the land will either bring a blessing or a curse. The Father's House team found old newspapers and books that carried many of the secrets of the city of Portland. Many of the characteristics that were established by the founders have created the opposite spirit of the kingdom.

THE GENERAL OVERVIEW OF TRENDS OF THE HISTORY OF PORTLAND:

The trends detailed below include the history of abortion in Portland, injustice, discrimination, homelessness, crime; but there have also been righteous trends that occurred throughout the decades. These only capture a piece of the history behind Portland, as they do not touch on all the foundational issues, nor do they even scratch the surface for the potential wells of revival beneath the darkness.

- Before any colonization, the indigenous people in Oregon were the FIRST to practice abortion and also practiced slavery.
- Portland started the first private abortion clinic in the late 1800s before it was fully legal in the United States. This clinic was located on a floor in a Portland Hotel, located where Pioneer Courthouse Square currently stands. "The Oregonian reported twenty-seven abortion trials in Portland during the fifty years between 1870 and 1920." [2]
- William Overton, called a "mysterious drifter" was one of the founders of Portland.[3] Overton was known for his lack of commitment; he was prone to wander, found himself always looking for the grass to be greener on the other side, and struggled to stay rooted in Oregon. For unknown reasons,

2 Helquist, Michael. The First Fifty Years of Abortion Trials in Portland ... - Ohs. Oregonian - OHQ, www.ohs.org/research-and-library/oregon-historical-quarterly/joel-palmer-award/upload/Helquist_Criminal-Operations_OHQ-116_1_Spring-2015_p.pdf.

3 Wicks, Chelsea. "Where We Live: NW Portland's Overton Street." KOIN.com, KOIN.com, 20 June 2016, www.koin.com/news/where-we-live-nw-portlands-overton-street/.

Overton left Oregon, and in the early years of Portland's establishment, even sold the land to two other founders. Overton's characteristics have manifested into the current generation and culture, where creatives often struggle with commitment and fear of missing out, especially in the northwest region.

- Portland was the second highest sex trafficking city in the country for decades. As it was known as a "port city," it soon became the center of gang activity from when it was first founded. Portland brought in miners and loggers and shortly after, the city was called to be one of the most dangerous cities because of the activity that occurred underground.
- The Old town area of Portland had some underground tunnels used for a variety of reasons that connected to the docks from bars and hotel basements.[4] The underground was used for extra storage from businesses upstairs, kept material out of rainwater, and was an easier way of transportation from the docks. Nevertheless, illegal activities occurred such as human trafficking, gambling tables, gang hangouts, and prostitution areas keeping women in tight prison cells. Those who were passed out or drunk were the targets. Bars were the main spot for kidnapping where the kidnapers known as the "crimps" would pay the bar owners to hit a button that would send them through the trap door. It came to a point where there was a shortage of sailors because they had been "Shanghaied" as men were kidnapped and sold on ships that were shipped out across the seas to a life of slavery at sea as crewmen. Portland has a rough history of hidden criminal activity. [5]
- Witchcraft and the occult, masonic roots, and new age practices have a deep history in the foundations of the land.
- Racial Injustice - People of color have felt displaced in Portland since its inception. When Oregon became a U.S. state in 1859, it was the only state that would not allow black people to live, work, or own property until 1926. This contributed to the low percentage of non-whites in the Portland area

4 Bruschi, Richard. "The 'Shanghai Tunnels' of Portland, Oregon—Kidnappings and Forced Labor in the City Centre." History of Yesterday, 1 Dec. 2020. https://historyofyesterday.com/the-shanghai-tunnels-of-portland-oregon-kidnappings-and-forced-labor-in-the-city-centre-8e1a660b0db.

5 "Portland's Shanghai Tunnels." Atlas Obscura, 21 June 2013. https://www.atlasobscura.com/places/portland-s-shanghai-tunnels#:~:text=Stories%20can%20be%20found%20about,about%203000%20people%20a%20year.

today. The Ku Klux Klan also carried a heavy influence in Portland, and it was common for businessmen to be involved as members. Vanport, a city between Portland and Vancouver, Washington, was once Oregon's second largest city before it was destroyed by massive flooding. Vanport's original purpose was to house war workers from WWII temporarily.[6] When the war first occurred, Portland was the only city on the west coast that did not have public housing for war workers. A large percentage of these workers were black. Even though the black community were allowed back in Portland in the 1940s, many whites still carried a prejudice mindset. From there, Vanport was birthed and land was acquired north of the city limits between the Columbia and the river's main channel to place the workers. Vanport soon became the largest US public housing project. In 1948, the Columbia River flooded, destroying Vanport and leaving 18,000 people homeless — mostly the black community on the streets.[7]

- Homeless issue: Today, the homeless crisis has been at a breaking point for some times, as it is one of the most visible problems when entering the PDX area. The sight of people living on the streets of Portland did not become common until the mid-1980s. This was caused by the inflation of the economy during that time (MacGillivray, 2021). Many mental institutions closed during those tough times and left people self-medicating on the streets.

Portland is known as the city where the homeless vacation. Many of the homeless today are not hungry, as sometimes you may see groups grilling burgers on the side of the street. The overflow of nonprofits with mental health and drug treatment programs, soup kitchens, and temporary shelters make these seem like the solution. Yet, the deeper issue of mental health is not being provided for, even though millions of dollars have been spent on the problem. Many wonder where the money is going, since the number of homeless continues to increase and drug abuse is just getting worse. When driving or walking throughout the Portland metro area, you will find tents on every corner; but checking back a different week you find the tents have been located elsewhere since the city does sweeps and

---

6 Toll , W. (2003). War Housing and Vanport. Oregon history project. Retrieved March 11, 2022, from https://www.oregonhistoryproject.org/articles/war-housing-and-vanport/#.YivaN3rMLIV

7 Geiling, Natashia. "How Oregon's Second Largest City Vanished in a Day." Smithsonian.com, Smithsonian Institution, 18 Feb. 2015, https://www.smithsonianmag.com/history/vanport-oregon-how-countrys-largest-housing-project-vanished-day-180954040/

clears camps periodically. These sweeps often scatter the homeless and they go elsewhere, or the same groups come back weeks later to camp. Before the pandemic, there were less than a dozen camps in various locations, but post pandemic, it has increased to hundreds of camps throughout the Portland metro area!

Some results from lack of taking care of the issue include homicide crime increase, with 533% increase of homicides in 2021 compared to 2020 (National Fraternal Order of Police), dumpster fires, mental illness spiking, naked people running around, leaving the streets trashed and scattered with used needles, human feces on the streets, and people high on drugs screaming and jumping into the streets randomly. What the residents of Portland often notice is that the homeless often don't bother people walking around the cities and won't usually attack strangers, but more often than not go after the other homeless camps with aggressive street behavior, pimps, drugs, and rape; leaving those who live in the area or come to visit feeling unsettled and concern for their safety.[8]

GENERAL RIGHTEOUS TRENDS OVER PORTLAND:

- Portland Revival in 1905 — stemmed from the Welsh Revival
- John G. Lake — Healing rooms in Portland 1926

John G. Lake, a leader in the Pentecost movement known for running healing rooms and planting churches, moved to Portland, Oregon for a short time in the 1920s. He had a vision of encountering an angel during a walk through Mt.Tabor Park in Portland.

Revival Prophecy for Portland, Oregon: Cindy Jacobs at Bible Temple in 1997:

"And the Lord would say to this city, 'I'm going to raise up the watch that will come from the city, and the anointing from this watch will be the anointing to break New Age.

'I will tear down the idolatry to humanism, and the Word will go out in the spirit that no longer will this be a haven for New Age,' says God, 'because I'm going to turn it around. I'm getting ready to manifest myself as the God of glory in this city. I'm going to release a river of miracles.

'I'm going to release signs and wonders. I'm going to cause limbs to grow where there are no limbs, eyes to be grown where there are no eyes.' And God says, 'I will even astound the medical profession.' And the Lord says, 'There will even be a day,

8 MacGillivray, Don. "History of Homelessness." *The Southeast Examiner of Portland Oregon*, 28 Apr. 2021, https://www.southeastexaminer.com/2021/04/history-of-homelessness/

even to this church, that you will see doctors line the platform, and you will see them come and you will see the crutches pile up, and you will see the wheelchairs and the stretchers, for I am doing a new thing,' says God.

'I will cause this city to be raised up as a standard. I will be on CNN News. I am going to not only heal bodies, but I'm going to heal this city,' says the Lord. 'I am going to heal the economy. I'm going to make out of this city a model that many people from governments from around the United States will be flying in, because I am causing a new anointing to come on this city.'

"And the Lord says, 'They will marvel because I'm going to be glorified in city government. I'm going to be glorified in the health and human services. I'm going to be glorified in the social services. I'm going to heal the educational system. I'm going to heal the legal system. I'm going to transform this city,' says God, 'and I'm going to use it as a model for America and the nations.' Over Portland we prophesy the miracles. We say the trumpet of the Lord is going forth in Jesus' name."

I find the year Cindy Jacob prophesied this significant because I was born in 1997. Before I was born, God knew he would send me to Portland when I was twenty to see the agenda of hell fall and to witness breakthrough and revival released over Portland!

We as followers of Jesus reverse existing unrighteous trends by releasing kingdom values over the land. Heaven and hell both need the agreement of men. If we don't agree to heaven's intentions, our silence will give hell a foothold.

While prayer walking or mapping, more than likely there will be things discovered that need to be uprooted as you read about. However, transformation over cities is a process. This process may look like mapping the land, prayer walking, taking care of those in need, building, and serving. Serve the city where you live.

You might not know where to serve until you map. Serve and build at these broken places. Serving releases favor to bring heaven to earth in areas of influence, allows the light of God to infiltrate people and places, and restores broken places. Isaiah 60 talks about how the glory of God rises in the midst of darkness but Isaiah 58 is our responsibility and the action steps for the glory to come. Heaven is waiting for us to partner with rebuilding the ruins. Building looks like serving in the local community outside of the four walls, prayer walking with a team, worshiping over these areas, taking care of the homeless, infiltrating the mountains of influence with kingdom strategy (government, education, etc.), and serving where there is a need.

Isaiah 58: 6-9 *"Is not this the kind of fasting I have chosen: to loose the chains of
injustice and untie the cords of the yoke, to set the oppressed free and break every yoke?
7 Is it not to share your food with the hungry and to provide the poor wanderer with
shelter— when you see the naked, to clothe them, and not to turn away from your own
flesh and blood? 8 Then your light will break forth like the dawn, and your healing will
quickly appear; then your righteousness will go before you, and the glory of the Lord
will be your rear guard. 9 Then you will call, and the Lord will answer; you will cry for
help, and he will say: Here am I."*

Verse 8 explains what will come after *loosing the chains of injustice, setting the oppressed free, sharing food with the hungry, and clothing the naked: "Then your light will break forth like the dawn, and your healing will quickly appear; then your righteousness will go before you, and the glory of the Lord will be your rear guard."*

The glory comes after the rebuilding and serving. God desires for the righteous to occupy territory to extend this Kingdom and bring it into its destiny. Don't sleep on spiritual mapping. It's an important key to bringing transformation.

STORY OF BEING CHOKED

As an intern, I served alongside the youth pastor, created kid's content and curriculum, led evangelism outreaches, collaborated with other ministries, and sent out weekly blog emails.

I spent most of my days as an intern at Portland State University at the park blocks across from where we attended our Sunday service gatherings, and where our church's offices were located. The park blocks are a central area where many students walk through in between classes.

A few weeks after settling in, one morning I left the church offices to go for a walk at the park blocks and call my dad to update him on life. As I was on the phone, walking past one of the dorm room buildings, I felt a pull to go in a certain direction. As I walked through an alley alongside one of the dorm buildings, something strange started to happen.

Out of nowhere, I felt a hand grab my throat and choke me. Through the phone, my dad noticed that I couldn't finish my sentence. He immediately knew something was up.

"Victoria! Victoria! Are you okay?"

I tried to talk but nothing came out. Tears flooded my eyes, but nothing came out of my mouth. Something was trying to silence me, but the campus was empty with no one around. I began walking back and forth trying to catch my breath, hoping the grip on my throat would release as I was still on the phone with my dad!

Finally, after a few minutes, the hands released from my throat, and I told my dad what I had just experienced. After I let my dad know I was okay, got off the phone, I immediately ran back to the office and told my pastor about my encounter. He asked where I experienced the choking, and explained that in the past, they took a team to that area, prayer walked it, and did prophetic acts in that very location to strategically remove darkness where magic and witchcraft was being practiced in the dorms. Steve seemed very familiar with what I dealt with earlier in the day as it did not seem to faze him.

The following week, Steve put me in charge to lead a prayer walk at that same spot. This was a defining moment for me. I had the choice to run away, yield to fear, and not lead the prayer walk or I could go to the spot where I was attacked and allow the Spirit of God to give me courage.

Each Wednesday our church teams up together in the streets called "City Transformation teams" with three strategic teams: prayer walk, homeless outreach, and power evangelism.

Throughout my time in Portland, various experiences similar to this one surfaced, triggering the kind of fear that easily paralyzed me, and I was given two choices: to be overcome by fear and the unknown lurking in the atmosphere; or ask for help from spiritual mentors, declare the Word of God, and call on the name of Jesus.

So, the following week, I chose to lead the prayer walk. As I went with a team, I shared my encounter from the previous week. I felt encouraged to have a team of people to back me up and pray against any continual attacks. Stepping onto the ground once more, I experienced intimidation, but I prayed over the area anyway and knew I was covered. I moved forward and confidently led that prayer walk. This was a threshold, a testing moment, and I stepped over it.

Key #2: Fear might present itself in the air but we have the option to come "under it" or "overcome it" with the power of Jesus.

Psalm 91 is my Scripture passage that I found myself leaning on during times of "in my face" spiritual warfare. I still go back to this and lean on it frequently.

When you abide under the shadow of Shaddai,
you are hidden in the strength of God Most High.
He's the hope that holds me and the stronghold to shelter me,
the only God for me, and my great confidence.
He will rescue you from every hidden trap of the enemy,
and he will protect you from false accusation
and any deadly curse.
His massive arms are wrapped around you, protecting you.
You can run under his covering of majesty and hide.
His arms of faithfulness are a shield keeping you from harm.
You will never worry about an attack of demonic forces at night
nor have to fear a spirit of darkness coming against you.
Don't fear a thing!
Whether by night or by day, demonic danger will not trouble you,
nor will the powers of evil be launched against you.
Even in a time of disaster, with thousands and thousands being killed,
you will remain unscathed and unharmed.
You will be a spectator as the wicked perish in judgment,
for they will be paid back for what they have done!
When we live our lives within the shadow of God Most High,
our secret hiding place, we will always be shielded from harm.
How then could evil prevail against us or disease infect us?
God sends angels with special orders to protect you wherever you go,
defending you from all harm.
If you walk into a trap, they'll be there for you
and keep you from stumbling.
You'll even walk unharmed among the fiercest powers of darkness,
trampling every one of them beneath your feet!
For here is what the Lord has spoken to me:
"Because you loved me, delighted in me, and have been loyal to my name,
I will greatly protect you.
I will answer your cry for help every time you pray,
and you will feel my presence
in your time of trouble.

I will deliver you and bring you honor.
I will satisfy you with a full life and with all that I do for you.
For you will enjoy the fullness of my salvation!" (TPT)

I know what it is like to be silenced and choked by demonic forces of darkness. But all the pressing and the spiritual warfare has awakened and strengthened my spirit-man to release my roar and unapologetically carry authority in Jesus. Hell is terrified of the Jesus that lives inside of those who believe in Him.

Since I have lived in the Pacific Northwest, there have been moments of seeing hell come after me with lies, confusion, and attacks. These moments of directly stepping on the fear that once gripped me has given me greater authority to bring VIOLENCE to the kingdom of hell by releasing the POWER and AUTHORITY of Jesus Christ on the earth.

This kind of *violence* I talk of is inspired from Matthew 11:12 which is interpreted as "*been forcefully advancing*" (NIV footnotes). "From the days of John the Baptist until now, the kingdom of heaven has been subjected to violence, and violent people have been raiding it." Matthew 11:12, NIV

Key #3: What you are "feeling" might not be you.

You might have the gift of being a "feeler" like me. The enemy wants you to think feeling is a curse. At certain moments, I have personally experienced the weight of the heaviness of Portland on my shoulders each time I left my house. It took some time to understand how to release that weight and ask the Holy Spirit to help me discern what I was feeling and understand what to do about it. These feelings might be originating from places, spaces, or people. The enemy is the prince of the air and wants you to think something is wrong with you. Discernment is an incredible tool to help navigate atmospheres when our feelings don't align to the Word of God. The feeling gift doesn't have to be a curse if you are postured correctly; your gift can transform into spiritual authority and discernment.

God may speak to you, through you, and show His presence in various ways through:

- Word of God
- Prayer/Worship
- Peace

- Healing
- Circumstances
- Wise Counsel
- Word of Knowledge/Impression
- Visions
- Dreams
- A familiar voice
- Through other people (could be encouragement or prophetic words)
- In practical signs-closed or open doors, numbers, words, etc...
- Supernatural manifestations

Word of knowledge: Is a revelatory gift given by the Holy Spirit that leads to facts and information about an individual's present or past that one may not know otherwise. This kind of knowledge may surprise someone since it may not have been revealed up to that point. The goal for words of knowledge is for the receiver to have a deeper revelation that God sees them and cares about their situation.

For example: birthdays/ anniversaries, street names or places, experiences, images that are representing true facts of a person's life.

Impression: Can be a feeling, type of perceiving; can lead to a word of knowledge for someone as you further dialogue with the Holy Spirit.

Prophecy: Is a supernatural partnership and activation that comes from receiving a revelation from the Holy Spirit and communicating out loud what the Holy Spirit is saying to encourage, build up the body of Christ, and bring forth what He is doing.

The purpose of prophecy and the revelatory gifts are to reveal the heart of the Father and to awaken sons and daughters into their call and purpose with the end goal of pointing to Jesus. However, love must be the driving factor when prophecy is released. It all must come from love and portray the heart of the Father.

It is in your nature and DNA to hear God's voice. When you declare out loud and prophesy:

- It releases the Word of the Lord;
- Through the agreements of your decree, you are binding and loosing on the earth what is already been bound and loosed in heaven;

- It brings understanding and application what the Father is saying;
- It demonstrates the weightiness and power of God when he speaks.[9]

INVITING JESUS INTO THE WORKPLACE:

It might be easy to approach a Christian friend and give them encouragement or a prophetic word, but what about in your workplace or in your neighborhood? The supernatural lifestyle doesn't have to stop within the four walls of the church. It is the sick that need healing. As followers of Jesus, we carry the authority to heal the sick, raise the dead, cleanse those who have leprosy, and drive out demons. (Matthew 10:8) We also have the HOLY SPIRIT, the greatest spiritual mentor who gives us insight on hidden things.

You carry more authority than you know to shift atmospheres, heal the sick, and bring the presence and peace of God everywhere you go.

When I worked for a company several years ago, my workplace carried a heavy atmosphere where it was hard to thrive in that kind of environment. One co-worker explained to me she defined herself as an atheist after I shared a bit of my radical lifestyle as a Christian. A couple months later, she came up to me and said, "I had a dream God told you all my secrets." I couldn't help myself; I lost it and bent over with laughter! This same woman who said she did not believe in God just had a word of knowledge about me having a word of knowledge about her! Throughout my time working with her, I had received different words of knowledge from God about her, but I sat on them and waited for the Holy Spirit's timing. The words I received about her touched-on pain from her past and even dark places she found herself in. I never shared this information to her or anyone else, but I believed God gave me this insight to intercede for her salvation and to give her grace as I worked through her tough personality. Words of knowledge are not always given to us so that we can "spill the beans." God may be revealing information to help us understand the individual or give us creative ideas to help them experience the love of God.

One of my favorite healing encounters in the workplace happened when my boss, Lisa fell and sprained her arm and encountered the presence of God when I prayed for her. A couple days after she received x-rays and returned to work, our office hosted an event. Between appointments there was a brief window to talk to Lisa as she walked to her desk. I thought to myself, "This is my moment to see

9 Material taken from Advanced Prophetic Training – Ty and Daneen Bottler Ministries https://www.tyanddaneenbottler.com/

if she will let me pray for her!" I quickly walked to her and asked if I could pray for her arm. I already knew Lisa called herself a Christian, but I would not have known otherwise as she was often swayed by atmospheres and the troubles of the world. We both were wearing white lab coats over our clothing, and I began to pray as I put my hand on her arm. After I finished the prayer, I opened my eyes and I watched a flood of tears drip down Lisa's nose and face. She looked at me and grabbed my hand and said, "Do you know there is healing power coming out of your hands?"

I chuckled and said, "Yes I know! That's Jesus healing you and touching you right now!" Lisa experienced heat from my hands being released into her body through two layers of clothing on. Her arm felt better after I prayed for her. Now that is my Jesus!

You are probably going to receive spiritual insight about someone; it could be the junk in their life-their sin, or struggle. Wait for the Lord to act on it. Discerning the timing of the fulfillment is important. Prophetic understanding and discernment are not given to pick out the junk in people. You might discern something "off" in someone but that does not give you the authority to call out the junk.

When discerning spiritual information, ask the Holy Spirit: "Do I say it, pray it, what do I do with it?"

Practical insight on navigating atmospheres/workplaces/neighborhoods:

- Be aware of how you woke up- before you left your house- how did you feel?
- Check in with your body when you go places (eg. headache, tiredness, fear, anxiety, sick
- Dialogue with the Holy Spirit about your day
- Invite the Holy Spirit and declare the word over the location (house, workplace, or neighborhood)
- Speak in your prayer language, release worship music in the workplace if you can
- Prayer walk your _________ with a buddy or a team who understands spiritual authority and ask God what He wants to release over the workplace.
- Ask the Holy Spirit what kind of demonic spirits He wants to remove and replace it with.

- Be open to receiving spiritual information about the space as you pray over it.
- Talk to a spiritual mentor to go over what you believe you discerned after the prayer walk. Ask to be covered in prayer.

TEAMS FROM BETHEL

During my church internship between 2018-2019, we invited Bethel School of Supernatural Ministry (BSSM) students from Redding, California to partner in outreach with our church. During evangelism outreach, we had strategic ways to reach students that opened a door to meet Jesus, whether it was through worship in the park blocks or signs that said, "spiritual readings." This might sound like New Age activity, but many Portland State students were prayed over through this approach, and they encountered Jesus as the BSSM students shared words of knowledge only God would know about them. Words of knowledge invite people to experience how God sees and knows them, giving them a chance to have a relationship with the God who personally created them.

Another fun way to reach campus students during the BSSM outreach was having a table with various pictures on it, letting people pick out the one that was highlighted to them. On the back, we wrote Bible verses, encouragement, and even a word of knowledge. I enjoyed the many times the BSSM students from Redding drove up and flooded the Portland State University campus.

DIVINE ENCOUNTERS WITH THOSE INFLUENCING THE KINGDOM

One of my favorite coffee shops in Portland is Heart Coffee. You might just find yourself sitting next to an influential writer or speaker in this Scandinavian, minimalist space.

The downtown shop is in the heart of Portland. First thing to know, is that they have a house-made walnut-almond milk, and the coffee flavor is on the lighter, fruity side. The price of the coffee comes with the bougee atmosphere. One morning, I grabbed coffee with a spiritual momma at Heart Coffee. As we ordered, I immediately noticed that an author and former pastor at a well-known mega church in Portland, sat at the other side of the shop. I immediately got a download from heaven — a potential word of knowledge — and felt led to encourage him with it. Boldness arose in my heart, and I walked right up to him. I introduced myself and explained how I was connected with Pastor Steve and that I felt led to share a word with him regarding his church. I noticed he seemed more at ease once I shared that I was connected to Steve and served under Father's House. The man responded with how he had seen the kingdom work Father's House has been pioneering in the city and wanted to know more what we as a congregation were up to. I remember the word I gave him had something to do with transition and receiving wisdom on next steps. He received it and shared that his church had some big decisions to make in the future. I felt relieved and sat back down with my spiritual momma. She told me how proud she was of me for fearlessly speaking up.

EARLY SPRINGS OF REVIVAL- SEPTEMBER 2018

The month I arrived in Portland, an incredible event involving the collaboration of more than a dozen churches was taking place at the Oregon Convention Center. It focused on bringing revival, evangelism, and discipleship to Portland. This event stirred up a movement and revival with the power of the gospel

Chris Overstreet, the founder of the organization Compassion to Action, had a vision of revival breaking out in America and the first location where that happened was Portland, Oregon. Chris's vision for the event was to see a revival and mass salvations springing forth in the Pacific Northwest, where people of all ages preached the simple gospel, seeing people set free, healed, and delivered. This vision formed a backdrop for the three-day conference event called "Portland 2018."

The speaker lineup consisted of powerful ministers:
Reinhard Bonnke
Daniel Kolenda
Bill Johnson
Ben Fitzerald
Todd white
Scott McNamara
Richie Seltzer
Marilyn Hickey
Lisa Bevere
Band: Steffany G., Upperroom, Lindy Conat, and Jeremy Riddle

It was incredible to see the churches in the Pacific Northwest join to contend for the city of Portland. I met a lot of incredibly fiery people at this event. After each of the sessions, teams would go out strategically and evangelize. The event did not just stay in-doors, but hundreds of us hit the streets. There were so many of us on the streets evangelizing that several people I encountered mentioned that other people had offered to pray for them earlier. The power and love of Jesus flowed through the streets of Portland!

During one of the outreach times at the conference, many of those who attended met near a central walkable area called Pioneer Courthouse Square. I met a Bethel student there who was also attending the conference. I chatted with her for a bit, connected on a deep level, and we continued to interact throughout the next few days of the conference. After one of the sessions ended, we went back to her hotel to rest, journal, and recover after the last few long but powerful sessions. We decided to journal near the elevators on her floor, as there were comfy chairs there arranged near a window. We turned our chairs around to look out at the window with a stunning view over the city.

After a few minutes, I heard an alarm sound from the elevators. I was so focused writing in my journal that the noise did not bother me too much, but I decided to turn my head, move my chair towards the elevators, and see where the noise was coming from anyway. The moment I moved my chair, my jaw dropped as I saw Steffany Gretzinger, a Christian music singer, songwriter, and former singer at Bethel. She must have been preparing for sound check as the conference was just a across the street from her hotel. At that point, Steffany was just a few feet away from me pushing the elevator button waiting for the elevator. I jumped out of my chair and said "Hi!" I don't even know if I said an encouraging word or what because it all happened so fast. But I did get a selfie with her. She was super gracious, humble, and relational. A few seconds later, her personal assistant and daughter, named Wonder, walked up to me and said, "Come on the elevator with us." It was so precious. I almost jumped on the elevator just to be with them, as Wonder almost convinced me to do, but it probably wouldn't have made sense if I did. There was no need to go on the ground floor with them because I would just come right back up to the floor I was on. I think God set the alarm off to let me know Steffany was there. I would have completely missed her if the alarm had not gone off because my chair was turned around away from the elevators. Thank you, Jesus, for the alarm! What a fun encounter!

POWER + LOVE OUTREACH ENCOUNTERS

During one of the evangelism outreaches at Portland 2018, I walked in a park with a group near the Lloyd Center not too far off from the conference center. A couple in the park were highlighted to me and I felt the need to share with them a word of knowledge about their business.

I went up to them and said, "Hey do you guys own a business?"

They looked at me and smiled. "Yes, we do!"

I said, "God told me that you guys have a business and I believe that He is going to provide for you and a miracle is coming your way! I just sense that maybe there are financial issues going on, but I want to reassure you that He is working behind the scenes."

The couple smiled and said "Wow that's amazing! Yeah, we have a business!" They also shared that they were from the conference too and were out evangelizing as well. The couple explained they were having issues with their business space, and they weren't sure if they were going to get kicked out from their landlord. It was a brief conversation and we all left encouraged. We ended up getting each other's contact information, even though I figured I would probably never run into them again. The next day, I received a text message from them containing a screenshot of a phone displaying the time and phone call log. With the photo was a message explaining that apparently, I walked up to this couple at the same time they received a voice message from their landlord telling them they could keep the space. God is funny. Even those who go out evangelizing for the lost, who believe in God, still need encouragement and confirmation sometimes. This was reassuring that I was growing in hearing God's voice and receiving words of knowledge for those I encountered in the right timing. I have learned that it is best not to think too hard about words of knowledge, or delay in obeying the prompting to share them, but just go out and take the risk in order to encourage people and help them encounter Jesus. If I had waited to share that word outside of the time I felt led to, who knows what would have happened? Maybe the couple could have answered the phone, but maybe they just needed encouragement and a sign from God that He was working on their behalf BEFORE the breakthrough arrived.

One of my favorite evangelism and healing encounters from Portland 2018 occurred when a team of friends and I walked near the Target in downtown Portland. We encountered two ladies and noticed one was walking with a cane. We stopped them and introduced ourselves. We briefly shared how we noticed them and spoke about the power of Jesus to heal people in pain because of His love for us.

The woman allowed us to pray over her. We laid hands on her, as her friend stood next to us. About a minute into the prayer, the friend, with tears in her eyes, began shouting, "I'm healed! I can feel my feet and my hips!"

I opened my eyes and my jaw dropped as I tried to comprehend what had just happened. The woman who we DID NOT lay hands on received healing in her feet and hips as the numbness in her body went away. She began to dance and joyfully jumped up and down. I had never experienced or seen anything quite like it. Jesus healed this woman without us knowing she needed healing or laying hands on her. I wondered why God did not heal the woman with a cane that day but healed the woman who looked physically fine from the outside. Our God is mysterious. It is best is to be obedient, show up, and let Him do the rest!

One lesson I have learned when praying for healing for people is to not stop at healing, but to allow those you encounter to meet the God who healed them. It's incredible when people receive healing through prayer. Healing points to Jesus, so give those you encounter an opportunity to meet their healer. Healing opens the door for a relationship with Him. Creating an opportunity for people to build a relationship with Jesus is the goal to keep in mind while evangelizing, rather than have lots of "healed" people end up in hell because they didn't give their lives to the God who healed them.

TAKE THE RISK

> **Key #4: Exercising your prophetic gift means taking a risk you might be wrong sometimes. Spiritual gifts grow through exercising them the way you would a muscle.**

When it comes to growing in discernment and exercising our spiritual gifts, sometimes it means messing up, taking risks, and accepting that you might not always get it right. The best way to grow spiritually is to find a safe space with mentors to bounce off ideas, take risks, fail, and learn what not to do from your mistakes. There were many times where I stepped forward in evangelism or words of knowledge, took the risk, and ended up being wrong, or the person did not receive healing as expected. Often, these people still encountered Jesus and felt encouraged.

As followers of Jesus, we are not in charge of who gets healed or who receives salvation, but we do have an obligation to preach the gospel!

He said to them, "Go into all the world and preach the gospel to all creation. Whoever believes and is baptized will be saved, but whoever does not believe will be condemned. And these signs will accompany those who believe: In my name they will drive out demons; they will speak in new tongues..." Mark 16:15-17, NIV

Scott McNamara, founder of "Jesus at the Door" explained the idea of evangelism in a practical way. "The Father, through the Holy Spirit who blows like a mighty wind, is shaking the trees and drawing men and women to Himself. Some apples will fall, some will move a little, and some won't move at all. All we have to do is be there to catch. As I went out onto the streets one day, the Holy Spirit said to me, 'Scott, imagine people on the streets are apples on a tree. You share, then I'll shake.'"

After the 2018 event, my fire for the Lord stayed lit months later. I took a friend out evangelizing to encourage her to exercise her prophetic gift. There is a powerful exchange when one surrounds themselves with other Spirit-filled believers who also walk in the supernatural. I have seen it time and time again, where we spur on and activate one another. Proverbs 27:17 (NIV), says, "As iron sharpens iron, so one person sharpens another."

My friend and I went to Whole Foods to purchase groceries and we were open to discovering who the Holy Spirit wanted to speak to while there. One of the workers was highlighted to me. She looked to be in her early twenties, and I immediately noticed that she was pregnant. I received a download, grabbed my friend, and went for it, double-checking to make sure she was pregnant. As I mentioned the encouraging word, I also acknowledged she was pregnant. The strangest thing happened right after that. The moment I said "pregnant" out loud, her pregnant stomach slowly went away, and I could see that she was not actually pregnant in the natural! I realized I made a mistake as her eyes got big. I noticed her demeanor change as if shame and fear rose up in her. I apologized right away, but the encouraging word I spoke over her made her cry and it touched her powerfully. She gave me the biggest hug showing how the word affected her. After that encounter, my friend said, "Victoria, I wanted to slap you when you shared about her being pregnant but then right behind her I noticed prenatal vitamins on the aisle!"

I'm not sure if this gal was recently pregnant and maybe was carrying some shame about it, or she may have been birthing something in the spirit. In the end, and what is most important, is that this woman encountered the love of Jesus and the power of the Holy Spirit as I encouraged and prayed for her. Sometimes the words of knowledge we share might be wrong, but what's most important is to create a space for the Holy Spirit to move. That may look like encouraging and loving the individual. It's hard to get it wrong with an encouraging word. Most people won't reject encouragement.

Other times you might ask them a question that you feel led to ask. Some people will lie to you or hide their emotions. What you see in the natural and on people's faces is not the most accurate way to determine what is happening. God may be encountering them in their heart, but they might be hiding it on their face. Other times, people just can't hide their encounter with the Holy Spirit moving inside of them.

My friend who tagged along at the grocery store later said, "I notice you carry a lot of favor. People have a hard time saying no to you even when your word is off."

This still holds true today even in the practical!

STRONGHOLDS IN THE LAND

As I walked the ground of Portland, I found myself confronted with the many layers of spiritual warfare, whether it was a physical attack, a battle within the mind, the atmosphere, thoughts of confusion, insanity, or push back through encounters with people. I learned some nuggets on Ephesians 6 just by standing on the front lines, and also through sermons from our senior pastor. Pastor Steve released a whole series on understanding the levels of darkness to defeat their works and how to stand wearing the armor of God. He broke it down and explained in depth what each spiritual force was and the type of authority they carry to understand how to defeat them.

These sermons and front-line experiences have helped me navigate what kind of spirit I may encounter, whether it is a demon, stronghold, or ideology.

Luke 10:19 explains that as followers of Jesus, we carry the spiritual authority to tread on scorpions. The Bible explains that demonic powers of authority were created beings, but one-third of this angelic host fell and rebelled against God. (Revelations 12:4) However, God made man, at this time lower than the angels, to have authority over their power. While the devil may have powers of authority under him, Heaven has angels who partner with us as we prophesy and release the word of God over nations, cultures, neighborhoods, and people. All the enemy has created is a counterfeit to God's original design. If we are given authority over these demonic powers and rulers, the demonic beings must obey under the name of Jesus. These demonic powers are under different categories that carry distinct powers and assignments.

Key #5 "There is a point where heaven knows you and hell knows you. The devil doesn't have greater power than us but he runs his kingdom on strategy. We must run on strategy too!" — Steve Trujillo

"Put on God's complete set of armor provided for us, so that you will be protected as you fight against the evil strategies of the accuser! 12 Your hand-to-hand combat is not with human beings, but with the highest principalities and authorities operating in rebellion under the heavenly realms. For they are a powerful class of demon-gods and evil spirits that hold this dark world in bondage. 13 Because of this, you must wear all the armor that God provides so you're protected as you confront the slanderer, for you are destined for all things and will rise victorious"— Ephesians 6:12-13, TPT

The NIV translation, in verse 12 , calls the entities "**rulers**, against the **authorities**, against the **powers of this dark world** and against the **spiritual forces of evil** in the heavenly realms."

You don't want to mess with these forces of darkness unless you are "known" and directed by the Holy Spirit with a team and confirmation to back you up. I have personally learned from prayer walks that demons sometimes can just be distractions. There are always going to be plenty of distractions, but where is the Holy Spirit leading us in these moments? There have been plenty of encounters with strangers yelling at me for no reason, and there are times where it is an assignment to focus on, and other times where that is simply a distraction. It's important to stay focused on your assignment, be covered in prayer leading up to it, go with a team of people, and to never go on an assignment alone.

(To learn more on the various demonic powers and how to stand up against them, listen on Spotify to the series *Overcoming all the Power of the Enemy*. You will find the series under Father House City Ministries and the title of podcast series that begins February 11, 2021.)

THE STRONGHOLD OF FEMINISM IN THE FAMILY SYSTEM

When I first arrived in Portland, I noticed the drastic difference between the west coast family dynamic compared to the east coast. I eventually identified one of the strongholds and ideologies behind the bizarre family dynamic in Portland: Feminism! In North Carolina and Virginia where I lived before, I found myself surrounded in a culture where couples often marry between the ages of eighteen and twenty-two, either directly out of high school to their high school sweethearts, or while in college following the "ring by spring" route. This kind of pressure is put on both men and women living in the east coast and southern culture. However, I wanted to get married young anyway, so I was okay with this pressure. From what I experienced, the men in the south often honored their mothers and wives, and encompassed the nuclear family dynamic.

When I moved to the west coast in the middle of my junior year of college, I took time to grieve that I was potentially giving up that desire for a season as I moved across the country and settled into a new city. However, I did not realize how much the west coast family cultural dynamic affected me. I noticed the cultural shift immediately and I picked up on the hopelessness and fatherlessness over the land that influenced relationships and marriages. As I observed the culture of Portland, I encountered more single people than married, who found themselves lost and still single in their late twenties, early thirties, and even early forties. My immediate reaction was "What did these people do wrong to delay their marriages?"

After three years of living out west, I concluded that the delay in marriages may have to do with multiple reasons: agreements in the land, agreements with people, generations, and the culture. However, I am confident God has a perfect timing for aligning marriages, but sometimes we get in the way through agreeing with what the world has to say about marriages rather than walking in God's original design for marriage. We may not be able to control when our spouse comes into our life, but we can control how we prepare to be a husband or wife, even if it seems far off. There are some things one can control when it comes to relationships that may affect future generation lines. The problems in the current generation and culture include commitments issues, gender identity confusion, lack of honor, consumerism culture with online dating, and divorces sky rocketing. As someone who is not native to Portland, it seemed to me there was some sort of "curse" over relationships and marriages in this region as many got married later in life. I wrestled with the idea and wondered if I would be one of those who got married late in life too. I hoped this wasn't the case so I decided and declared from day one that my future husband was not going to carry this orphan mindset, deal with commitment issues, or come under the culture's twisted definition of love, and that this curse from feminism would not influence my marriage.

The people living in this area have two choices: to come under the spirit released over the region, with the women in dominant role carrying a rebellious attitude, or the other option — come in the opposite spirit and believe in God's original design of family over the region. I wrestled with watching friends struggle in relationships, and I even struggled finding my person as well. I kept noticing a pattern that many men do not know how to pursue or honor women; the roles were switched. The roles seemed to be switched in feminism culture as it silences men and their role as the protector and has twisted the definition of manliness. Not all marriages I witnessed were like this in this region but many that represent the feminist culture resembled this.

Marriage is designed to represent God and his bride. Family is such a precious treasure that flows into culture and society, and every mountain of influence streams from it. For example, education may influence kids, but the family mountain shapes a foundation for the child's future and generational line. The same goes for media and arts and entertainment, but if parents neglect giving their children wisdom and truth founded on biblical principles, the demonic ideologies released from the media and education mountain will be the child's main source of truth. **God's design over the family mountain pioneers and creates a standard for the culture. Families represent the kind of strongholds or blessings that are over the land.**

This ideology of feminism on the west coast culture did not appear overnight. It established itself all the way back in the pioneering and gold rush days which points to why the ideology is stronger on the west coast. When families headed out west on the Oregon trail, a lot of the men died on the trail because they took the greater risks of hunting and fishing. Because of that, the woman had to carry on the man's role without men. This created an unintentional "independent spirit." The enemy used that as an opportunity to twist independence and created unintended consequences that hurts the family mountain. Feminism has become a counterfeit of God's original design.[1]

Feminism has taken over the men's role on the west coast which has created a lack of manliness in the family system, causing boys to be more feminine than the women. Feminism is founded on a lack of mothers and fathers from the experiences on the Oregon trail, that led to a manifestation of rejection from deep generational wounds. These deep wounds then trigger acts of rebellion. At its core, feminism replaces God and the earthly father's role by replacing them with a counterfeit. The ideology of feminism may seem harmless, even useful as a good cause, but it creates pretensions in arguments, fosters partiality, and even carries the potential to destroy family roles and the role of womanhood. The values, agreements, and partnerships behind feminism are out to delay marriages and destroy the family system that God put in place.

---

1 Podcast by Victoria Kent. https://youtu.be/Ae4FM5x7cLU- reference ("CTI Podcast: Episode 1: The Agenda Behind Feminism is Destroying the Family Mountain")

Feminism looks more extreme in Portland compared to other cities. I asked a range of people who live in Portland what feminism looks like here, and what kind of language was used in the culture. Some responses included:

- Portland used to be known as the city of beauty, "City of Roses," but this person pointed out now feminism has brought in exploitation, anger, vulgarity, and opened the door for pornography to become normal through the artwork here.
- Others here in Portland notice that if a community of individuals are feminist, they most likely will associate themselves with new age practices, support or be heavily involved in the LGBTQ community, espouse Marxists values, and be radically pro-choice.
- During the summer riots in 2020, we saw "Mothers in Helmets" on the news associating with, and protesting standing tall next to extreme groups like antifa at the late-night protests at the Portland justice center where riots went on for over 100 days.
- Outward expressions that we see a lot here: women walking around not shaving their legs and armpits, naked bike parades (both men and women)
- Open-sexual orientation in children's books and nipples shown as trendy abstract artwork
- If you are a woman business owner in Portland, you are more than likely a feminist.

FEMININITY > FEMINISM

One can be feminine in style, but they don't have to associate themselves as a feminist. Just because a woman is a business owner, it does not mean she has to bow under the ideology of feminism. I tackle this stronghold of feminism through declaring God's truth and promises over families and coming in the opposite spirit. I wear femininity and royalty intentionally in my clothing style to express my creativity and personality. I have had individuals come to me thanking me for wearing a dress or pink because it is so rare to find. I pray for sons and daughters under the orphan mindset to receive revelation on God's original design of the family system.

What sons and daughters under the ideology of feminism spiritually crave, although they may not realize it, is:

- To feel wanted and accepted

- To have the opportunity to invite fathers and mothers to partner with us to heal and mend our hurts towards one another.
- The power and revelation of God to reverse the counterfeit and negative fruit of feminism that is affecting families and future generations.
- For women and men to take their place in how God designed them to be. Women crave for men to be the protector and defender. This leads to intimacy and connection that brings healing to hearts.
- Men crave to be honored and supported by their wives as they defend their family.
- Humans ultimately crave intimacy with God. Marriage forges a foundation and opportunity to receive and understand the Father's heart.

I have felt the push back and the attack as I have spoken out against feminism. I have even had dreams where the spirit of feminism suffocated me. I choose to stand out against feminism and bring light to the agenda behind it—the attempt to destroy the family system. I choose to believe that God is awakening hearts and calling sons and daughters back into their alignment with who they are designed to be.

DREAMS THAT POINTED TO MY ASSIGNMENT TO GO AFTER FEMINISM

I have had a series of dreams over the years that points to my assignment to align daughters stuck in extreme feminism and homosexuality to find their true direction and identity in Christ.

I had a dream that broke the fog and curse over those partnering with the spirit behind homosexuality. The dream started with me outside of a house with names of people on the roof. These names were friends and acquaintances I met in various years and seasons of life beginning in college. Each person represented a different season of my life. One gal in the dream wore her wedding dress. In real life she is married but she had a couple of very close girlfriends, including one who secretly was attracted to the same gender and has recently come out. Four of the women in the dream were a group of girls from my college who did life together and lived on the same dorm floor. In real life, only one of them has had a boyfriend and been married so far. In the dream, one woman was the one releasing confusion to all the other women who were straight.

As the dream continued, I found myself in the same room as these women, but I was undercover. The woman in her wedding dress, who is married in real life, was contemplating her marriage and seemed sad and confused. I could tell that there were unhealthy soul ties and bonds — mostly unperceived — between the women. The one bringing confusion about sexuality to the others knew what she was doing and intended to convince the other women to live as lesbians. All the women in the room started dancing and saying curses, the way one would entering a college sorority group. They had no idea they were releasing curses in the air and coming into agreement with their choice of language. I began to speak in tongues the same time they released curses. Soon enough, my tongue language became louder than everyone else's words and they heard me. Suddenly, all the girls except the one who started the curses looked at me and slowly backed away. The woman with the wedding dress said, "WOW! I feel the peace and fear of God right now!" It was as if the curse was lifted, and they could see clearly again. I woke up soon after that.

The next day at church, a friend of mine said to me, "Hey I invited a friend to church. She is not saved. Can you save a spot for us?" I ended up sitting next to this guest. The moment I met her, I sensed that she had a girlfriend. I welcomed her with open arms and in the middle of worship, I felt the Lord moving in her heart. I tapped her on the shoulder and said, "I just want to let you know I am so glad you are here! I know it can be intimidating coming to a new church, but so glad you made that decision to come today! I also wanted to let you know that right now you might be feeling heat or peace over your body and that is Jesus moving in your heart." She lit up after I shared that with her, and she gave me a big hug. A group of us made her feel special and took her out to eat sushi after church. At the lunch table, she had a lot of questions and wanted to hear our testimonies and was hungry for more. She even shared with my friend that she was not sure if she believed she was gay anymore because she was having second thoughts that maybe she wasn't as attracted to women anymore. That blew me away that she so quickly questioned whether or not she was gay anymore!

PORTLAND- HALLOWEEN CENTRAL

My experience in Oregon has opened my eyes to the reality that witchcraft is praised in the culture in the Pacific Northwest, and made me realize I can no longer support celebrating Halloween.

There are various normal, "hipster" art shops I've walked into in Portland that have embraced witchcraft by selling brooms, tarot cards, crystals, and witchcraft jokes on paper cards, intermixed with normal trendy products all year long.

The artwork in the shops may look harmless because it's trendy, but in reality, it is deceptive.

What I find the most interesting is that one of the most popular bookstores in Portland, across from the Christian book section, carries all things related to witchcraft, pagan practices, magic, and how to perform real spells. Because of how open the new age practices are out here, I have avoided celebrating Halloween as it has opened my eyes to inviting spirits into my home and giving the enemy a foothold in a "fun" way. Halloween carries the spirit of death, and ever since moving out here, I have been cautious of attending Halloween parties and associating myself with the celebrations.

I usually will not attend Halloween parties unless there is a strategic reason for why I am attending. One year I was invited to a costume party in Portland where some Christian friends were in attendance. The host mentioned to me that there were a couple of people who called themselves atheists, and several of us were intentionally there to look for an opportunity to share the gospel. I introduce myself to the strangers who I knew were not believers. Not long after I arrived, a friend handed me a cookie. I didn't think twice about asking about the ingredients and grabbed a bite as I was socializing. After a couple of bites, my eyes got large, and I immediately ran to the sink to spit it out as I realized there was peanut butter in the cookie. In the past, I had multiple visits to the hospital because of eating foods with traces of peanuts. After accidentally eating a bite of the cookie, fear began to rise up in me as I tried calming down to gulp down water as fast as I could.

My friend, who was the host, immediately noticed that I started freaking out. She grabbed my shoulder and looked me in the eye and said, "Stop being fearful." Her words brought me back to reality for a moment. I walked outside to get some fresh air, and the gal who I was hoping to evangelize at the party was outside. She was super gracious and tried calming me down saying "You are going to be okay." Even though my throat felt like it was closing, and I could barely talk, somehow, I had the strength and confidence to tell her, "You are going to see Jesus heal me tonight." That was all I could say before I quickly ran to the bathroom to relieve myself.

I had remembered what a mentor had said. "Fear often lies in the gut." Something clicked in my spirit at that moment. As I was on the bathroom floor rolled up in a ball, I decided to call out my fear. I slowly got up, pointed at myself in the mirror, put my hand on my throat and said, "I command fear to leave my body in Jesus' name. I declare healing over my throat." After a few seconds, I removed my hand and noticed the redness from the allergic reaction disappear! My throat began to feel normal again and I could talk more clearly. Just a few minutes later, I walked out of the bathroom yelling, "I'm healed!" Most of the people at the party had seen miraculous healings before but they were all shocked as I went from hyperventilating to filled with peace. After that wild healing encounter, I chilled, grabbed some food, and watched a movie the rest of the night.

The one time I attended a Halloween party after moving out west, I received radical healing in my body!

Key #6- We carry the power to heal sickness and disease in Jesus' name

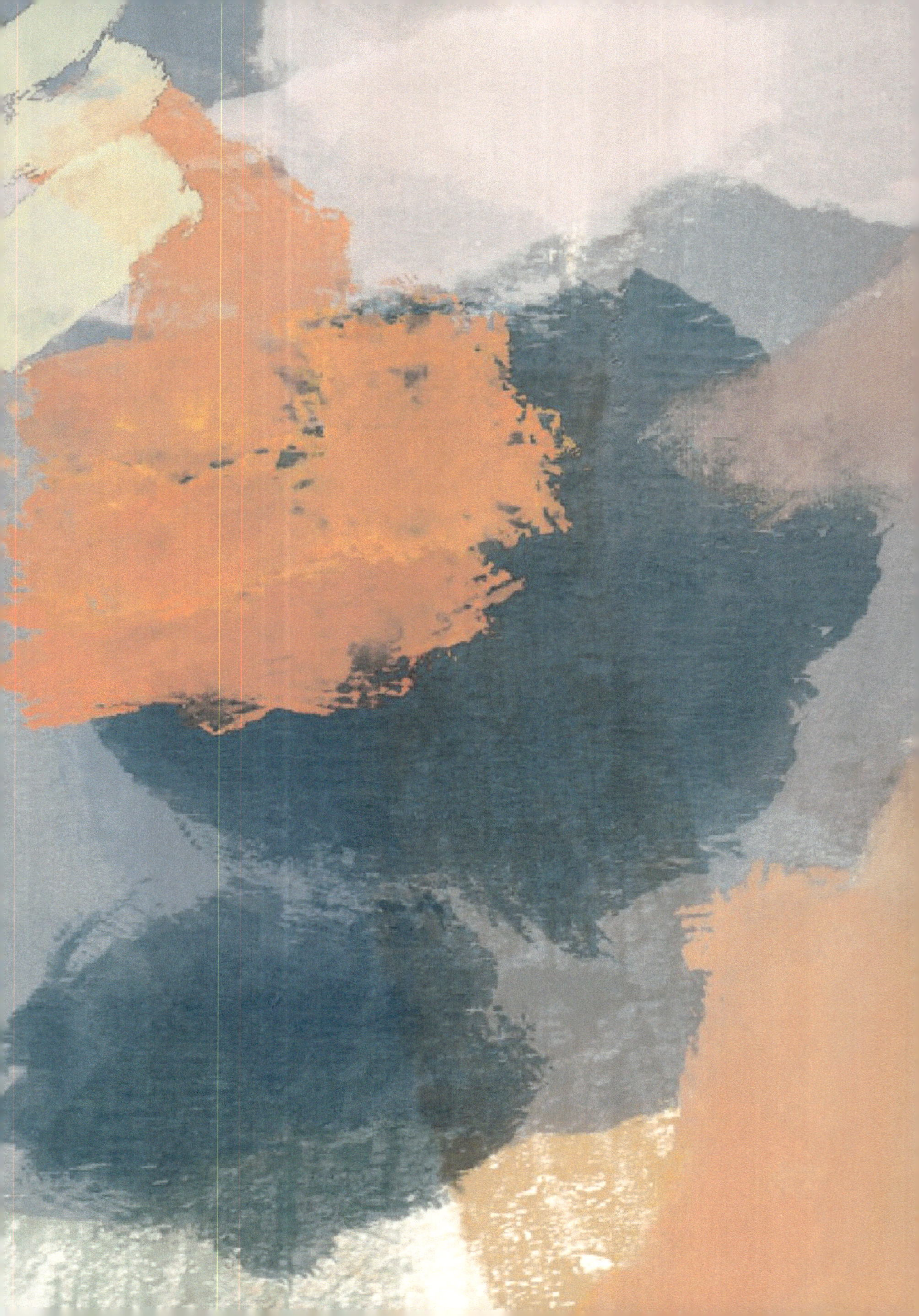

FRONT LINES OF HELL

In this chapter, I want to share four extraordinary events I witnessed that occurred in 2020 during the summer and into early fall.

1. 100+ days of Portland 2020 riots at the Justice Center.
2. Wildfires in Oregon, Washington, and California.
3. Saving Chinatown from looters.
4. 5,000-7,000 worshippers in midst of riots in downtown Portland.

WORSHIP IN THE STREETS OF PORTLAND > THE VIOLENCE IN PORTLAND

After the George Floyd incident, Portland became one of the top cities where rioting went on for over 100 days, with the news declaring that Portland was now up 1,600% in crime compared to other cities in the U.S. A large number of police officers quit in Portland because of the "defund the police" demands, leaving officers feeling demonized and chastised ever since the death of George Floyd.

Late one summer night during the peak of the riots, a group of strategic prayer warriors and I gathered around the Portland Police Bureau at the Multnomah County Justice Center. This was the prime location where the riots occurred. At these late-night demonstrations there was just a fence between the protesters and the police. The prayer team and I were there to prayer walk, gather spiritual insight, and dismantle the agenda of the enemy.

That night, a group of protesters were stirring up the crowd with the intention of breaking down the barrier and releasing the prisoners in the building. Our prayer team passed out donuts even as we began to dismantle the schemes of darkness and witchcraft and release the peace and presence of God over the chaos. This is what I described earlier in the book as going in "the opposite spirit." Walking around in this kind of atmosphere made me feel nauseous. I could not believe my eyes as I heard young people my age chanting and cursing the police. "Abolish the police!" "All cops are bastards!" I noticed most of these protesters were Caucasian, ranging in age from early high school to what looked like mid-thirties. Each night there would often be regular protesters, there for a good cause, but later there were others that would stir the crowd and create chaos and violence.

As I made my way to the most heated area to pray, the guy next to me had his phone out, streaming a live video as he interviewed a police officer on the other side of the fence. I called out to the other officers to come closer to the fence so I could pray for whoever I encountered. They all allowed me to pray! I had to yell as I prayed over all the chanting and the loudness of the crowd. I think my prayers were on the guy's live video!

As the team made a loop in the crowd, we noticed some people releasing sage in the air and we asked them why they were doing it. They told us they were cleansing the air. You could tell that a few minutes after the sage was released, waves of anger would come over the crowd and then it would calm down; this happened multiple times throughout the night. I could feel fear and anger in the air — some moments stronger than others. I noticed that those who were there to bring disruption and violence looked at me funny, even though we were undercover. It was as if the spirit behind the anger knew the presence we were carrying.

The same night, the peaceful gathering turned into a chaotic mess. Hours after the team and I left, one of the protesters threw some sort of firework over the fence at the police, an officer ended up being injured, and the wall between protestors and police officers was knocked down, leaving the streets open to lawlessness.

After my experience that night, I realized that it is not people we are fighting against, but demonic forces and strongholds that "build houses of thoughts" and false ideologies. This is a counterfeit of what true kingdom justice looks like. This kind of "justice" creates exhaustion from never being satisfied, building up anger and lawlessness, creating partiality in false agreements of justice that leaves others suffering in shame and guilt.

Key #7- We don't wrestle against flesh and blood but against spiritual rulers and authorities and cosmic powers.

It's not the people who are our enemies, but they can be influenced by demonic spirits knowingly or unknowingly.

WORSHIP WITH SEAN FEUCHT DURING SUMMER RIOTS

By August of 2020, Portland had been in the headlines for months with news stories of rioting, burning, and looting, grabbing the attention of Americans waiting to see what would happen next to the city of Portland.

On day seventy-three of unrest, worship leader Sean Feucht and local churches strategically partnered together. Saturday, August 8, five events happened on MLK Day. I started my day downtown to witness the presence of Jesus infiltrate the city of Portland with praise, worship, prayer, and evangelism. I took notes of the entire day and wrote a blog post from a newspaper perspective.

In the morning, starting at 6:00 a.m., prayer groups gathered in the city of downtown Portland. At 10:00 a.m., approximately 100 people attended evangelism training at Tom McCall Waterfront Park, led by Scott McNamara, founder of "Jesus at the Door."

Simultaneously, another evangelism training group gathered in Vancouver, Washington, led by Chris Overstreet, founder of Compassion to Action. By noon, both outreach groups flooded the public streets of downtown Portland sharing the gospel of Jesus. I got to lead a group of new evangelists on the street.

At 4:30 p.m., there was a national holy activism event: *Pray on MLK* at Peninsula Park in North Portland, led by the organization *Civil Righteousness* with the intentions of bridging the gap in forgiveness and creating a foundation for racial reconciliation.

For the finale event in the evening at Tom McCall Waterfront Park, Sean Feucht and a local Vancouver, Washington worship team from *Bethesda Church NW* created a space to gather people outside the four walls of the church.

The previous year, Sean Feucht spearheaded outdoor worship gatherings throughout America, ever since the California governor banned singing and worship in the state.

Sean Feucht, from Redding, California is a father, missionary, worship leader, founder of Burn 24/7, and former congressional candidate. In the past fifteen years, Sean has traveled all throughout the world and the Middle East, entering warzones, leading worship, and spreading the gospel. The warzone of Portland did not intimate Sean and his team from entering and inviting local churches to worship Jesus.

I wrote a blog post from that night, when the worship gathering in Portland surprised viewers as it changed the narrative from a city of riots to a city now known as a hotspot of revival. Approximately 4,000-7,000 people showed up to worship Jesus; many had not been able to meet inside a church for several months because of COVID-19 restrictions from Oregon Governor, Kate Brown. Many traveled out of town from southern Oregon, California, and Washington. Just a few hours after the worship event, we heard in the news that riots and a fire broke out inside the SE Portland Police Precinct.

One of Sean's songs from the album *Wild, "Till the Whole World Looks like Heaven,"* rings true to the worship movement sweeping across America. The lyrics read: *"We won't stop singing till the whole world looks like heaven."* August 8th was a pivotal moment for the church to step outside the four walls.

This event was not a typical Christian event, but rather an opportunity for the city of Portland to witness breakthrough as it ignited hope to rise above the fear and chaos.

Dr. Charles Karuku, one of the pastors who spoke at the George Floyd memorial, was a guest speaker at the worship event. Local African American worship leaders from Maranatha Church led worship for a portion of the evening with Sean, as church leaders from the Cascadia region united as one body of believers.

While many members of various political groups and activists came out of curiosity, many left with questions answered after conversing with outreach ministries. One young man was a Proud Boy activist; another told about his commitment to the BLM movement and LGBTQ causes. That night he received answers to his questions, and later was baptized at the Portland waterfront.

SEAN FEUCHT PART 2 - 2021

Sean Feucht came back to Portland a second time on August 8th, 2021. Those who attended the worship night a year before carried a different confidence and strategy this time, and were prepared for anything as they gathered to worship. Over sixty-five security volunteers acted as a barrier around the families worshipping. These volunteers included ex-military, ex-police force, and Christians from local churches who wanted to protect the people at the event and de-escalate any situations. This was supposed to be a family-friendly event. The attendees also couldn't help but notice the whole time that the Portland police were not present at all at the event from 4 to 9 p.m., nor later when things got out of hand from

9 to 11 p.m. Later, the word got out that there was a robbery and homicide that same night in the city that kept the police officers busy. Antifa observed the event from afar as they were outnumbered, but they did not attack those who attended until after the event when attendees split off into smaller groups and walked back to their cars.

The local news media portrayed that there were several groups that clashed that night: antifa and proud boys and Christians. But in reality, families were there to worship Jesus and gather with fellow followers of Jesus, to come in agreement for the city of Portland, to bring the presence of God where there had been chaos and darkness. The volunteer security guards were not associated with the proud boys.

I was located on the stage behind the musicians. During the event, antifa beat on drums and made noise from the outskirts of the crowd during worship, but the worship from the crowd and the musicians drowned out antifa's rage. I felt safer on stage but could feel the intensity surrounding me. Heaven and hell felt very close to my face. My friends and I raised our hands to Jesus amid feeling and seeing the corruption and anger just a couple feet from us. I noticed that one of the local leaders of the city on the stage with me kept looking up at a building, as he noticed someone with a sniper rifle on a high building. There were a couple of moments of yelling and watching security guards running back and forth as antifa tried to creep up in the crowd to attack Sean and the band leaders. At one point during the set, Sean said out loud to antifa "We know that if you are not worshipping and don't know the words, we know who you are." It was obvious who was not there to worship; the members of antifa stood out like a sore thumb. One of them who kept trying to slowly creep on stage, ended up giving his life to Christ in between the worship set. It was a beautiful moment as he surrendered his life to the Lord and wept. A flood of Christians surrounding him laid hands on him and prayed over the new follower of Jesus.

After a couple of hours, I remember my stomach churning, and I tried to discern if it was from fear or wisdom. Where I was located on the stage, I could see out better than on the ground where the crowd stood. After the offering, before it started to get dark, I felt led to leave and grabbed a guy friend to walk with me past the antifa crowd to the street closer to my parking garage. The event was not even close to being over, but I felt in my spirit it was time to head home.

As I walked to my car, I had this weird feeling in my gut that I just needed to walk faster. I walked to the dispenser outside the parking garage to pay for my parking, and realized I forgot my parking ticket in my car, so I had to walk back into the parking garage before I could drive away. I was annoyed at the delay. When I finally got in my car, I pulled out my phone and hung out for a few minutes. In the back of my mind, I still felt an urgency to get out of there fast. So, I tapped my directions into my phone and headed home, but strange things start happening. My GPS took me in circles, and I couldn't get out of the main waterfront area. Confusion was in the air, so I started praying and declaring confusion to leave. It took me about ten minutes to start heading in the right direction. It was as if I was under a fog of confusion. I remember feeling relieved after getting on the interstate and noticing the confusion and chaos lift.

A few minutes after I got home, I jumped in my pajamas and checked my phone, and noticed a missed call from my friend. I called her back and she answered by saying, "Are you alright? Did you make it home safe?"

I responded nonchalantly, "Uh, yeah I did. What's up?"

She told me that antifa had followed families back to their cars near the end of the worship night to intimidate people and release M-80 explosives! I left the event thirty minutes before the m-80s were exploded in the parking garage where I was parked! Families were attacked as they walked back to their cars. A mother and her baby got pepper sprayed by antifa.

A family with three kids experienced antifa up close on their way back and set the story straight as they reported the truth during a news report interview. As this family left the worship gathering, they heard some booms in the distance. They were told by others walking home to wait to go back to their parking garages because antifa was blocking the entrances, intimidating people and not letting them enter. The family waited for a moment and called a friend on the security team. While on the phone, they saw a clear path to get to the garage. As they were going up the stairs, they noticed a couple of friends and asked them to help with holding their photography gear and their kids. Suddenly, they heard someone shout "Get down; get down!"

A moment later, explosives went off and smoke filled the air, as the sound echoed through the parking garage. The family ran to their car as another bomb exploded right next to them.

One of the children said, "I have never been so close to fear before," but despite the chaos, they handled themselves amazingly well.

The wife commented to the reporter that their family attended this event to worship and that one should not have to worry or experience m-80 bombs leaving church.

The husband was asked by a news reporter: "What would you say back to antifa in response to what they did?"

He responded, "We love you. We have a lot of common values and desires—freedom, desire to have everyone be okay, and that is alright with us. As long as it doesn't infringe on the safety or rights of other people. That's fine, go ahead, you do you, just let us do us. However, I don't understand why you are protesting us except that you are coming under the narrative that has portrayed us in a certain way. Unfortunately, there have been bad actors in our camp that have perpetuated those stereotypes of who we aren't. We were allowing everyone into the worship gathering. We were only stopping any potential violence."

A couple of my favorite highlights during the worship included witnessing:

- Local Portland/ Vancouver pastors take time out of the worship set to join together in agreement and declare God's destiny over Portland
- A handful of people in the crowd give up their addictions as they threw needles, pills, cigarettes, marijuana, and blades on stage
- Watching people get set free, delivered, and baptized, crying out to God, contending for God to move to Portland
- Witnessing an antifa member cry out to God and receive prayer

The Church of Portland stands strong despite the intimidation. The territory of Portland is the Lord's.

SAVING CHINA TOWN

As COVID-19 laws shut down over 200 flourishing businesses in the Old Town area in the summer of 2020 — with residents still living in the neighborhood — homeless camps migrated to where social services were still available in Old Town. The number of tents in Old Town (China Town) increased exponentially. However, it was not just the homeless that came to the area, but also pimps selling girls, and drug dealers peddling their merchandise, often intimidating and abusing the homeless as well.

The few owners in Old Town that kept their businesses open returned to find broken windows and their business ransacked. On top of that, many tents blocked the entrance to businesses.

The Old Town streets were mostly deserted and filled with trash; hardly the place anyone would want to go shop. Both businesses and the homeless living on the streets found it difficult to face bands of marauders who came late at night to break windows and loot in the wake of the protest. This violence traumatized the vulnerable population of homeless folks, many of whom suffer with PTSD and mental illness. Old Town needed a turnaround.

As our church was already familiar with bringing the church outside its four walls into the streets, we decided to spend more time in Old Town on Wednesday to worship, prayer-walk, and provide resources for the business owners who were still open in the midst of the burning and looting.

One of the ladies on the outreach team had a powerful word and declaration for the area: "Old-town Turnaround"; and the name stuck. We believed that Portland was primed for a turnaround from unusual places. The outreach team established a mobilized and stationary approach in the Old Town District with prayer, worship, and a multi-pronged strategy to see things turn around, finding practical steps to help the business community and the homeless.

Located in Northwest Portland, Old Town was once known as a haven for the Chinese and Japanese communities in the 1870s. Slowly over time, it was significantly influenced by poverty and it developed into a homeless hub, with high drug use and crime, and mental illness highly prominent. This part of town near the Willamette River has had the nickname of "Slab-town" but is now being referred to as "Stab-town."

Before the state of Oregon imposed restrictive COVID-19 protocols in mid-March 2020, the Old Town neighborhood attracted tourists to the iconic features in the area such as the Portland Oregon Sign, Voodoo Donuts, Chinese Garden, many restaurants and nightclubs, and the legendary Saturday Market.

On the outreach expeditions, the Father's House team noticed some of the homeless would protect the business owners' shops. Several business owners stayed up at night carrying firearms outside their shop to watch for looters, as the police were being targeted and might not have been able to arrive as quickly if there was a break-in.

Neither the COVID-19 concerns nor the riots in downtown Portland held back our unified team as we continued to boldly come together in agreement, delivering hope and expectation to see neighborhood transformation through prayer and worship.

Several members from Father's House have built a relationship with the Portland city council and the Portland police to find a way to save the neighborhood of Old Town.

The teams ministered in the homeless camps with prayer, providing supplies, cleaning up the streets, and declaring life and blessing over the businesses, serving the business owners by helping with preparations for re-opening.

I felt it was important to write down what I witnessed as the team blessed the area of Old Town. I asked several individuals, "Why do you come to one of the most dangerous areas in Portland to sing and worship?"

Response #1: "To release the presence of Jesus who is the Prince of Peace. The Bible says that God is enthroned on the praises of His people, so our praise is enthroning Jesus over areas that have been under siege."

Response #2: "Jesus doesn't ask us to go where we are comfortable. He asks us to go where we are needed."

Response #3: "Now is the time for the church to be unified. We are given authority in heaven to shift the atmosphere and bring heaven to earth. Portland as it is in heaven."

Response #4: "We seek to unite the homeless and the business owners in caring for the neighborhood and protecting it from further devastation of marauding bands of looters by showing each of them how valuable they are to God, how He cares for people, but also their dreams, aspirations, and investments."

Key #8: Worship is our warfare that destroys the agenda of hell.

WILDFIRES IN THE PNW FALL OF 2020

Beginning of March 2020, our lives changed because of surprising COVID restrictions in the country; and the residents of Portland witnessing over 100 days of riots that kept us on our toes, watching to see if Portland would burn down. We never thought we would experience a different kind of fire. I'm confident that the entire community was tired from all the constant struggles. Late August and early September, wildfires began to spread throughout Oregon, Washington, and California. The Pacific Northwest witnessed an unprecedented account of fires, with more than one million acres burned. People sought hope, a refuge, and waited for the rain to drench the burning region. The bright orange and red sun hung in the distance. These deadly fires destroyed hundreds of homes and caused a mass evacuation.

These tough times inspired me to create a "PNW Revival Fire" t-shirt and donate five percent of the proceeds to wildfire relief. The physical flames swiftly moving throughout the region created a wildfire effect, which ignited a "spiritual awakening fire" in hearts to rise above the tangible circumstances. These supernatural winds blew a spark that landed in hearts and created a flame that cannot be snuffed out.

Let the heavens open and the rain drench the land of Cascadia.

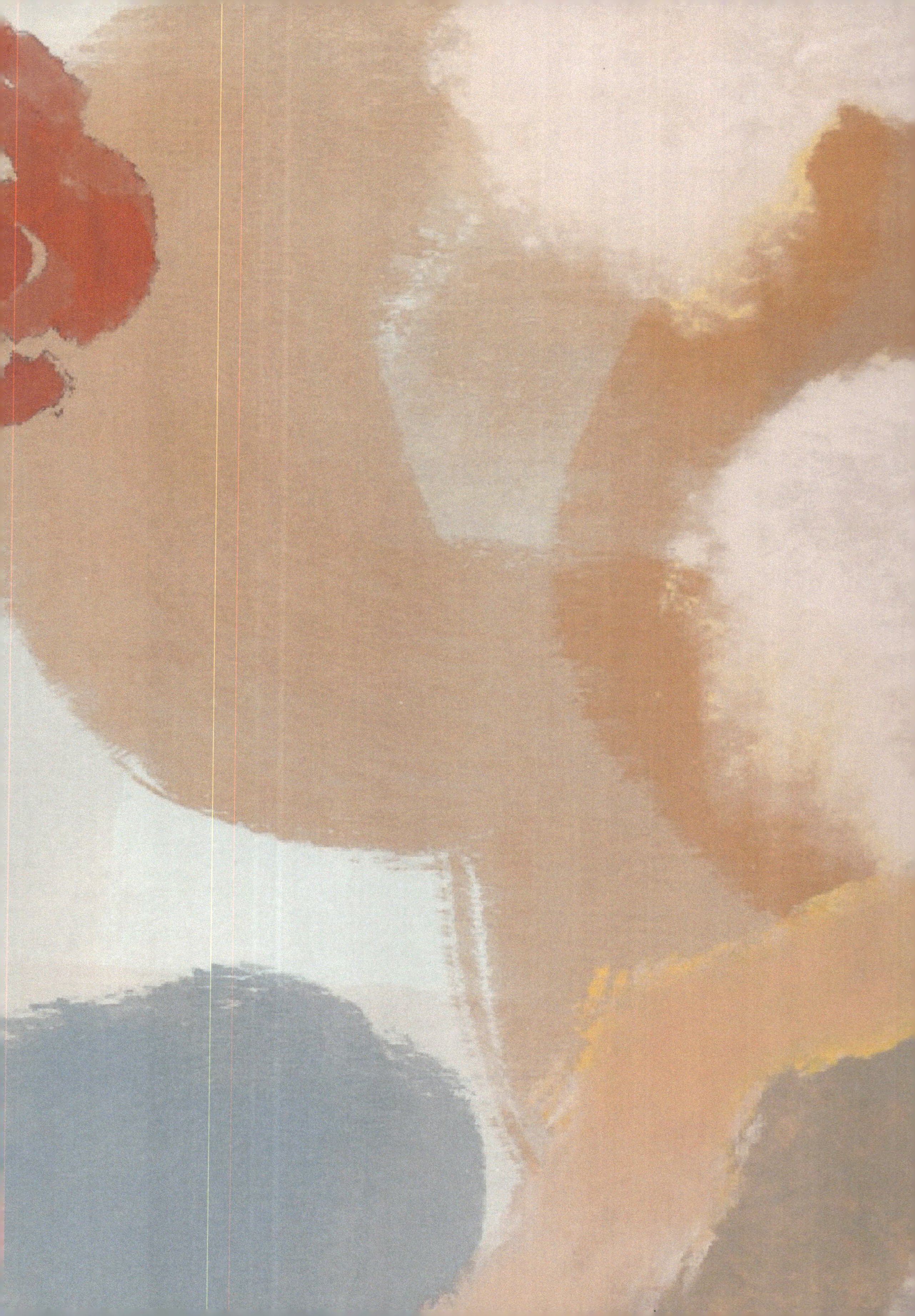

SPIRITUAL AUTHORITY

Sometimes greater authority is given after one experiences something firsthand. You might have to go through a difficult situation, and then in the end, you receive a greater authority to impact transformation and to reach others who may be dealing with the same kind of situation.

I never played with drugs or marijuana in my lifetime so could never relate to others who may have had a radical transformation from a drug addiction to finding freedom. But I saw firsthand many misusing drugs on the streets and knew I carried spiritual authority to pray for others, cast out demons, and even witnessed praying for someone to come back to their senses and be sober. But I really didn't know what it was like to be high. I had heard that Portland drugs seemed to create more intense hallucinations and paranoia in the users, compared to other cities. Portland is known to be a pool for illegal drug trafficking with a wide-open drug market.[1] You will hear about a time how God allowed me to experience a taste of what it was like to be high so that I could acknowledge and call out the stronghold behind the drugs and the reality of these strongholds keeping people in bondage.

In 2020, when the bill "Measure 110" was passed decriminalizing possession of small amounts of heroin, cocaine, LSD, methamphetamine, and other drugs, I immediately spoke out against it on social media. This bill called for less jail time, lower fees for being found with these drugs, and charges to be reduced from a felony to a misdemeanor.[2] If caught, the misdemeanor fine equaled the amount of a parking ticket and could easily be waived if the individual received a health screening from one of the local recovery hotlines.

As I boldly spoke out about this topic on social media, I received backlash and negative comments. The following day at my hair salon appointment, I started

1 https://www.portlandoregon.gov/police/article/735629

2 Reference: Murray , Krystina. "Oregon Decriminalizes Drug Possession." Addiction Center, 27 Sept. 2021, https://www.addictioncenter.com/news/2020/11/oregon-decriminalizes-drug-possession/

dealing with menstrual cramps. My hair stylist, whom I trusted, offered me a CBD gummy to relieve the cramps. I double checked to make sure there was no THC in it before I took it. I had CBD before in drinks and it just made me feel relaxed. Thirty minutes after eating the gummy I started feeling weird, my vision became blurred, and the world was spinning. At that point, the hallucinations got so bad that I got up to go to the bathroom in the middle of applying bleach to my hair. It felt like witchcraft and confusion — similar to other experiences I'd had downtown — but not on this level before.

I tried to speak in my prayer language in the bathroom and break off witchcraft, but nothing changed. I still felt the same. I realized I was high.

I tried to text my housemate, but couldn't even see the screen on my phone, so I was not sure if it went through. I wrote: "Someone gave me a marijuana gummy. I'm high. Can you pick me up? I'm five minutes down the street."

Before I left and got picked up, I let the hairstylist know that the gummy she gave me made me high. (Turns out I'm really direct and blunt when I'm high.) I soon found out that the gummy was homemade.

Thirty minutes later, my housemates arrived with their children and picked me up from this embarrassing situation. The moment I walked out to the car; the kids rolled down the window. "Victoria, are you okay? We came to rescue you!"

I felt like a zombie.

Once we arrived home, the kids fed me and offered vitamin C before I passed out on the couch. I was both hyper and mentally exhausted at that point. I tried to sleep, but my brain would not shut off. All I could hear was chatter coming from the spiritual realm. I heard lies whispering in my ear. However, it didn't feel like the lies were directed at me. I can't recall the exact lies I heard, but my spirit knew they were lies as I heard chatter in the air that felt like an assignment of death and confusion. It reminded me that Satan is the prince of the air. I thought to myself, "Wow this is a taste of what the homeless of Portland experience and those that rely on drugs. This is the curse over the land that keeps people in bondage." I had never experienced what it felt like to be high. Now that I have experienced it, I carry more authority to break off the waves of confusion and insanity over the land.

That night as I felt like I was going insane, strange things were happening in my neighborhood around the same time. I had always felt our neighborhood was quite safe, as we had a firefighter next to us with security cameras around his house. The next day, our neighbor shared what he saw on his surveillance camera. One of the neighbors at the entrance to the neighborhood had a restraining order against a woman, but that person violated the order and was roaming our neighborhood. The woman who lived in the house apparently stabbed the man who ignored the restraining order with a fireplace tool. The man wandered door to door, bleeding and asking for help throughout the neighborhood.. He left puddles and smeared blood on multiple neighbors' doors.

What a weird night! I got my money back from my hair appointment and never went to that hair stylist again.

Key #9: The spiritual attack may deepen your spiritual authority if positioned right.

That spiritual attack of feeling like I was going insane, in the end gave me greater authority to resist the spirit of insanity and speak to the trauma of mental illness.

FASTING >COVID

August 2021, I was believing for a breakthrough in my finances and for direction on certain relationships. The Lord directed me to fast coffee and go on a specific diet for thirty days. Before starting the fast, my normal routine consisted with including coffee in my day to focus on work or if I needed to process, coffee helped me relax. Drinking coffee was my false safety that I desperately leaned on. (It did not help my bank account either.) My housemates introduced me to a lifestyle of removing foods that contribute to inflammation, similar to the paleo diet but much stricter, called the autoimmune protocol. About halfway through the fast, my body felt good, I was clear-minded, and no longer craved coffee.

I was able to fast a couple meals throughout the thirty days which surprised me. Up to that point I had not been able to completely fast meals due to blood sugar issues, but my body was able to take care of itself without feeling dizzy or lightheaded. This was a good sign that my blood sugar levels were in a healthy place.

The couple who coached me told me to expect to go through a detox where my body didn't feel good. They shared that I might experience "flu-like symptoms" as the body releases inflammation. A week before finishing the fast, I started dealing with pains and aches in my hips and back. I assumed these aches were just the detox that I expected my body to go through. However, the pain lasted more than a week. It was so intense that I had ice all along my body to reduce the pain and inflammation; that relieved it as long as there was ice on me, and I felt the need to work out every fifteen minutes just to experience a few moments of relief. Movement helped but I had never experienced this kind of pain before.

After a week, it did not go away, and I started having a cough and sore throat. I eventually found out I had COVID-19. Not only did I ache, but I felt like I was losing my mind. I physically felt empty inside with loss of taste and smell, so food did not even satisfy me! It tasted horrible, even though I was hungry and longed to be filled up by something. I wanted to grab on to comfort food but, in the end, Jesus was the only stable thing I could hold on to. I found myself constantly pacing in my room because of hunger, but not being satisfied by food I couldn't taste. It felt like torment, death, and a familiar spirit that had tried to take me out before.

As I lay in bed surrounded with ice all over my aching body, I just had to let God fight for me, rest in His presence, and know He was taking care of me even if I didn't always feel His presence in that moment. A lot of the time during these few weeks, I was too tired to sit up and read my Bible, so I put it on audio and just lay in bed listening to the Bible. Worship music and the audio version of the Bible got me through those tormenting days. I could barely stand to cook, so I had to ask for help and have friends pick up and drop off food.

Sometimes breakthrough looks different than expected. The expectation of how I thought the fast was going to go really surprised me! I learned the process of resting. I started from warring in the spirit to resting and letting the Lord and all of heaven fight for me. I'm proud of the temple God gave me; it's stronger than I thought it was! I know that whatever the enemy tried to do to bring torment and disruption to my fast with the Lord, I will receive a double portion of blessing! I'm still not afraid of covid because the blood of Jesus is more powerful than any disease from hell!

Key #10: Rest in the middle of the battle and let the Lord fight for you!

GIVEN THE KEYS TO THE CHURCH BUILDING

During the first summer of COVID, our church spent the summer meeting in someone's backyard, because our location in Portland State was closed due to the pandemic. Throughout the year, we met at multiple places but did not find a home to settle in. We were all just grateful to see one another so we moved around wherever, but deep down we were ready to find a new home. We eventually found this incredible place and met in a coffee roastery for a couple months. Since it was not our space, we had to dot our i's and cross our t's with the COVID rules. After several months, we lost the space due to a potential outbreak and had to vacate in a week. We were back to square one — a church without a home. However, we used that time to our advantage and just did more church on the streets. On one city transformation night, we sent out a prayer team and asked the Lord His original intent for the land when that neighborhood was first created. When Father's House moves into an area, we begin to pray over the land and bless the land. An industrial area we prayed over was originally farmland, and the neighborhood transformed into mainly produce businesses today.

The prayer team knew that there were Christian food businesses before we ministered in that neighborhood. The team decided to bless the produce businesses to prosper during the pandemic. During one of the prayer walks, a lady witnessed one of our groups, and she loved that a team was praying over the neighborhood. Turns out the woman owned a couple buildings in that neighborhood, and was also a believer. One of the ladies on the prayer walk exchanged numbers with the owner of the surrounding buildings and shared how we were losing our current church space and asked if there was any space available.

Sony Pictures filmed a pilot series for TBS in one of the buildings, and they named the bar for the series "Like Father" at the very place Father's House was going to being meeting! The hundred-year-old building used to be a popular restaurant and bar. Before that it was a hotel.

When walking into the neighborhood, often you would see homeless people starting fires and dozens of tents surrounding the neighborhood, as well as cars being broken into. However, every Wednesday night during outreach, teams prayed over surrounding businesses and brought supplies to take care of the needs of the homeless. The atmosphere of worship and serving throughout the week transformed the neighborhood not too long after that, cleaning it up in the natural and in the spirit.

The Lord provided a home for Father's House for a season. Lots of glorious worship meetings and services happened in that building. One of my favorite moments was when a candidate running for governor of Oregon attended a service. His whole security team walked in, and the candidate sat in the second row, not knowing how strongly this service would impact him. That Sunday, we hosted a prophetic guest speaker named Bobby Haaby from Bend, Oregon. The first thing that happened after worship was that Bobby called up the young adults in the church and spent at least twenty minutes praying over us. One by one my friends got hit in the spirit, crying out to God and encountering Him, each in their own way. In that service, I could feel the weight of the generations before us cheering us on as we prepared to boldly take on the season before us, walking in the destiny God has for us.

Bobby then transitioned into calling out certain people in the crowd and giving encouraging prophetic words. He called out the candidate, referring to him as "the man dressed in a suit" before Bobby knew his name. Bobby had no idea who he was until after the service. As he received prophetic ministry, you could see tears running down his cheeks.

After the service, I walked up to the man and asked how he heard about attending our church and he explained that several of those at Father's House are on his intercession team. I thanked him for joining us. He said that he was bawling his eyes out the whole service. Something rose up in me to tell him that we as a congregation have got his back. I shared my love for Portland and that we as a church body are here to bring light in the city. I could feel the weight of this moment: what if he became governor? Portland would change for the better.

There was a beautiful exchange at that service on so many levels. These experiences are divine encounters. That service was probably one of my favorites because it gave me hope that when kingdom people partner practically and through prayer with government leaders who are open to heavenly strategies, it opens a door to heaven invading earth.

We occupied that building for a year and a half without paying rent, due to the generosity of the owner. When the time came that the church needed to vacate, through a series of divinely-orchestrated events Father's House was enabled to purchase a building for the first time in its history.

THE TIME I ALMOST LEFT PORTLAND

I traveled to Wales, the English countryside, and London in the summer of 2019 for a month with elders from my church to minister and educate churches on the topic of the "Ecclesia." I traveled right around the time I finished my internship at Father's House. At the end of the trip, I was having second thoughts about staying in Portland. I remember towards the end of my Europe trip sitting in a restaurant in London feeling confused, unsure, and overwhelmed by my thoughts. With tears in my eyes, I told the two people I traveled with, "I feel like the enemy is trying to kick me out of Portland!" We are going to pause here and come back to this moment. I am going to share with you my story of traveling to Europe and how the enemy crept in and used a good experience against me to bring confusion and chaos to try to kick me out of Portland.

There was something extra special about entering the land of Wales because my blood line has some Welsh in it. The three of us who went had incredible speaking opportunities, and Holy Spirit encounters as we trained people in evangelism and witnessed demons and spirits leave people. We also connected with a home base church there. I even went on a date with a Welsh boy.

Portland and Wales have a unique connection because of the rich history of the Welsh revival and Evan Roberts, the man who pioneered that revival in 1904-05. While I visited Wales, a group of us even visited the church that was the location of the famous story of Evan falling out of his pew saying "Lord bend me" after hearing Seth Joshua preach. Evan began to pray bold prayers, like praying for a hundred thousand souls for the Kingdom, and soon started putting on meetings where people were really encountering the Holy Spirit. repenting and fully surrendering their lives to Jesus, even though these meetings had no musical instruments and often no preaching. This revival fire in Wales spread to other countries and the U.S. It sparked a revival in Portland where 200 major stores and bars would shut down at a certain time of the day and people would hold prayer meetings! During our time in Wales, the main church we connected with had chairs from the Welsh revival that we sat on. It was sobering.

There was something unexplainable that spoke to my soul and it really drew me to Wales. The Bible college in Wales captured my attention as I heard the story behind Rees Howells, the man who founded the college. I found myself so captivated by the culture that I began dreaming of living there. I started making irrational decisions and was considering abandoning my assignment in Portland, as I was mesmerized by the land. I allowed something "good" to dominate my thoughts, and it ended up distracting me from the season God had me currently in.

I even filled out the paperwork to apply to the Bible college and was accepted. I was being driven away by fear of coming back to Portland and did not want to finish my current assignment on the west coast. From Europe, I went home to see family for a couple weeks to regroup. I did not even return to Portland immediately after the trip. I was shutting people out in my life during that time as I was so sure I wanted to move to Wales and be a part of the Bible College. During my time on the east coast, I felt like I was being tormented by not returning to Portland. My nine-year-old brother had a dream one night that demons were nipping at my heels and trying to mess with me, but that they couldn't quite touch me.

Hearing that from my brother gave me peace for what was happening in the spirit. There was so much confusion during that time. That week on the east coast, I walked into Trader Joes and bought some wine and the worker who checked me out asked for my I.D. and noticed my Oregon driver's license. He went off on how his family is from there and how he just loves Oregon. I remember being annoyed by his comments because I didn't want to think about Oregon.

I was running away mentally and physically. Luckily that same week, my sister wanted to visit Oregon, so she planned to fly there and needed me to go as well because she didn't know anyone else. A couple weeks later, we flew out to Oregon together, and I realized I made a mistake, so I apologized to those I needed to communicate with for leaving my assignment.

Key #11: Something good or an open door might not always be from God but could actually be a distraction or not in the right season. God is not a God of confusion.

In this situation, I opened a door for the enemy to come in and bring confusion over my thought life and it brought torment because I delayed in returning to my assignment.

My heart was pure in wanting to move to Europe, but God specifically rooted me in Portland for a reason and positioned me for such a time as this. I would have missed COVID-19, all the crazy rioting, and the radical worship that went on in Portland the following year! Thank you Jesus for bringing me back to Portland.

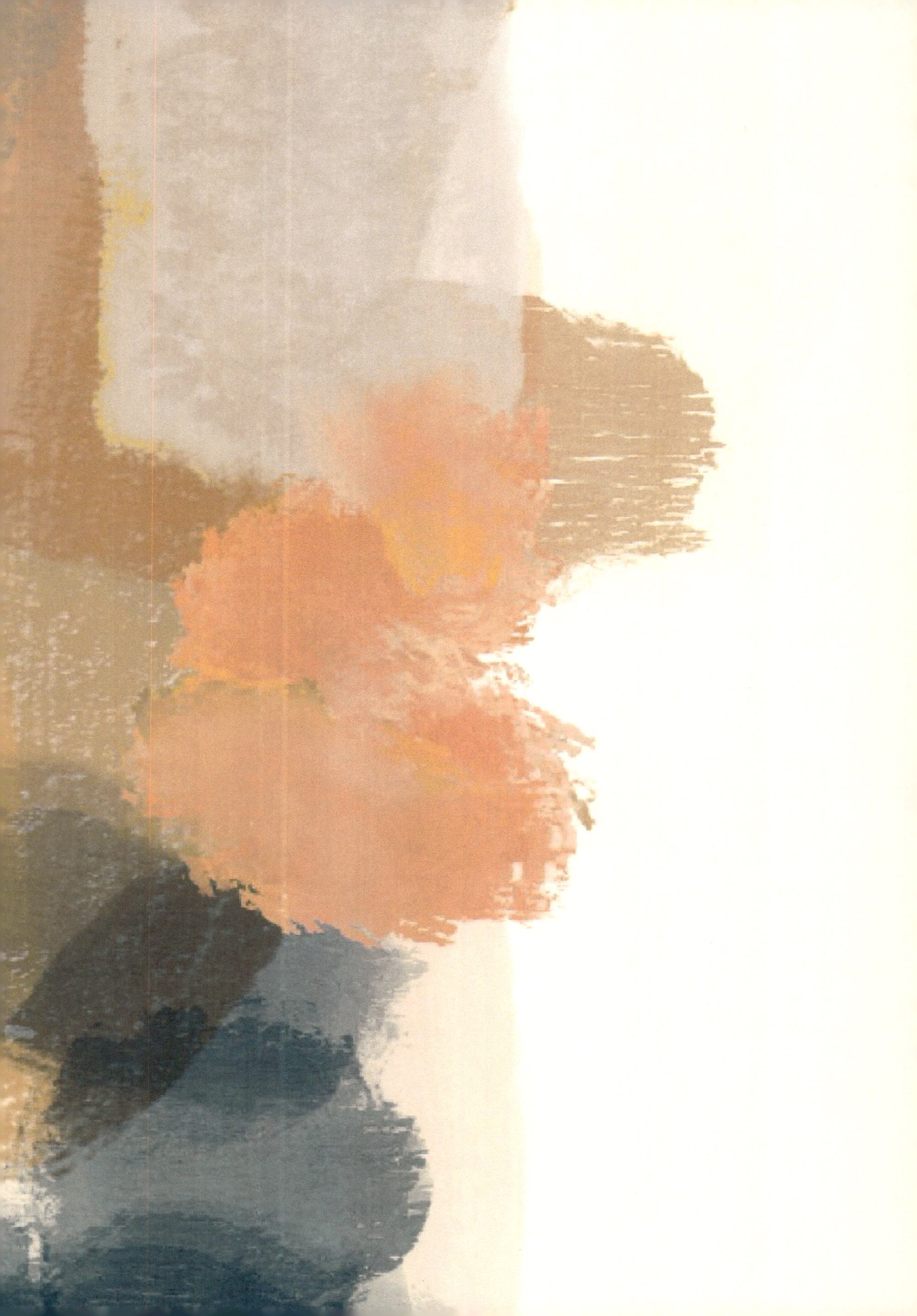

CREATIVITY + COLOR

My spirit awakened as I continued to live in Portland, surrounded with art plastered on the walls of buildings, walking into shops with local artisans, and stepping into the iconic Powell's bookstore with many local authors. This kind of atmosphere opened my eyes to grab hold of the creative blueprints of heaven and bring them down to earth. I thought to myself, "There must be even more than this for the city of Portland! Most of these creatives don't even know their Creator but their art points to Him whether they realize it or not!"

Key #12 Creativity is an outpouring of heaven flowing from inside of you.

Portland thrives on creativity, and I am confident that it was not random chance that the majority of those who live here are business owners, pioneers, and creatives in their own way. The people here value originality and uniqueness. They are even willing to pay big money for clean, bougee food, and clothes that are sustainably made or created by local makers.

The online "influencer" culture and the feminist activist culture have been magnets for each other in Portland. Before making my business "Called to Inspire" official, I attended a social media marketing event. The theme of the event focused on influencers in social media. Other local influencers from Portland were there. These influencers, both attendees and speakers, were mainly activists, creatives, entrepreneurs, photographers, and content creators. The guest speakers shared their journeys of how they became local celebrities. the top of being an influencer and local celebrity. As the speakers shared their stories, I felt the emptiness the speakers must have felt, as I sensed there was no authority behind their actions, but instead what seemed to be much striving to get where they wanted to be. And it seemed like an impossible goal for the rest of us. After attending the event, I was emboldened to communicate better to people that through Jesus we carry supernatural authority and influence. There is a difference between being an influencer vs. leading people to transform their lives, mindsets, and bring transformation to a culture. It takes spiritual insight and discernment to carry this kind of anointing and mantle to transform a culture. Attending the secular event gave me the revelation that one of my assignments is to equip ordinary people to become Kingdom influencers, so they are able to utilize their gifts and the spiritual authority they have been given to bring heaven to earth. If we are not invading and influencing the front lines of culture, who else is going to bring heaven to earth? We don't want the "spiritual authority" and "influence" put in the wrong hands.

THE PHOTOSHOOT THAT LAUNCHED CALLED TO INSPIRE

A couple months before March of 2020, I had a vision of curating a photoshoot, bringing influencers from the Kingdom of God that represented all seven mountains of culture. The idea of the "seven mountains" is language to help communicate the concept that followers of Jesus are called to be ministers to the front lines of culture. This definition of a "minister" may look different to a doctor, counselor, teacher, pastor, or business owner. The seven mountains are areas of influence in society and culture that will often embody a career. The seven mountains are Media, Business/Economy, Arts and Entertainment, Family, Religion, Government, and Education. As followers of Jesus, we have heavenly resources and all the keys of the Kingdom of God.

For the photoshoot project at the creative space, I asked the women I invited to wear a certain color that represented the mountains of influence they believed they were called to. These women had different assignments in their specific mountains. Yet, some of these mountains flow into each other; for instance, the business mountain funds all the other mountains. I wrote earlier about how the family mountain creates society and impacts all the surrounding mountains. This extraordinary and colorful photoshoot captured the importance of inviting Kingdom leaders to flood the front lines of culture. It was the most beautiful experience.

We shot in this space just a couple of weeks before we knew of COVID, and the world shut down. The woman who represented the family mountain brought her baby with her. The woman who wore green and represented the business mountain flew all the way from New York to take part. Altogether I invited ten women, and had seven women at a time represent the seven mountains. The dreamy Portland location captured all the vibes on my check list: the minimalist look, the green plant props, and movable color walls.

The photoshoot was a turning point for me. At that point, Called to Inspire was just a blog and a website but stepping out and carrying the hat as a creative director for that project, opened my eyes that God had bigger plans for Called to Inspire as it eventually turned into a business a few months later. Living in Portland with creativity and color inspired me to release my creativity. If you would have asked me years ago if I was creative, I would immediately have said no. I never quite felt confident in typical forms of creativity such as painting or drawing. However, my creativity sparked when I moved to Portland through outlets such as hosting, curating spaces, graphic design, creating atmospheres—and through excellence. In my first year of college as a freshman in 2016, I started my first blog. It had been on my mind in high school but I never pursued it. In college, the thought kept coming up so I decided to pull the trigger. The blog focused on topics that people are often hesitant to talk about: redefining cultural language into kingdom culture. Other topics included: shame, modesty, shining the light of Christ in the darkness, evangelism; I even eventually wrote news stories that occurred in Portland from an eyewitness perspective.

I look back and see God's hand in Called to Inspire before the business even existed. It is truly beautiful how God gently spoke to me through visuals, through words of encouragement and words of knowledge from others, and even how my brain works through creativity and aesthetic styles.

In the winter of 2019, right before 2020, the Holy Spirit continued to speak to me in pictures through creative visuals. I kept envisioning outlines of faces that looked geometrical. Rainbows were another image that kept coming to mind. My business logo is a rainbow and one of my first clothing designs ended up being seven geometric outlined faces that had various subtle color throughout the design.

As I traveled back to the east year for a short time to visit family during the Christmas Holiday, I found myself entering divine appointments. One Sunday, when I attended Catch the Fire in Raleigh, NC, a stranger came up to me at the service and gave me a word. "Tap into your creativity. You cannot be put into a box. I see lots of yellow. Big things are coming."

At one of the Father's House services the guest speaker, Chris Overstreet, and his ministry team prophesied over those in the service. I received a word about receiving blueprints from heaven, graphic design, and starting a clothing line.

What I have learned about prophetic words is that words may not always just fall into your lap. Divine appointments may happen, yes, but you must position your heart and take action regarding the words you receive.

PROPHETIC WORDS BIRTHED INTO REALITY

Growing up in a Christian school, wearing modest clothes was inevitable for me.

The guidelines were helpful and were set in place for a purpose. Somehow, years later, I was still hiding under oversized clothing. I dealt with some body shame, so I covered up more than enough. I understood the freedom and authority I carried in Jesus and how He freed me from condemnation and shame.

But walking in the complete fullness in modesty, I needed the supernatural hand of God to save me. I believe the download I received for clothing designs was so much greater than just a clothing line, but it gave me the freedom and authority to set a standard to wear royalty as sons and daughters. It may be cliché to say this, but what people wear is often a mirrored reflection of how they see themselves and feel about themselves. I came to the realization that even though I may have felt shame for having long legs, other's opinions about my body did not have to define me anymore. God made me perfectly and wonderfully, and in time, with input from friends and family who pointed out my struggle with wearing oversize clothes, I received more freedom from shame. I now wear clothes that fit me!

I spent six to eight months praying for the right graphic design artist to help me shape my ideas. I received encouragement from various friends who shared that God would provide the right artist who could partner with my vision.

I did my part and sketched out ideas but was not familiar with working on digital graphic design from scratch. I found myself frustrated with how to make my ideas a reality. I felt stuck as I knew a bit about graphic design but needed an outside perspective to achieve the brand look I desired.

God strategically orchestrated the story of how I met my current brand specialist! When I traveled to the east coast to visit family right before Covid hit, I stopped in at one of my favorite old stomping grounds: The Cure Coffee House in Norfolk, Virginia. While I sat at my table thinking about all the memories I made at this shop, I overheard two girls praying. I smiled and went up to them afterwards and shared how I loved hearing them pray in a coffee shop. I shared that I was visiting from Portland and how I used to live in Virginia Beach. As I further talked with the two ladies, I found out that one of the girls, named Abbey, and I had mutual friends. We exchanged Instagram information and stayed in touch. After a couple of months following her on Instagram, I noticed that she was a graphic design artist and she called herself a branding expert.

I reached out, and soon enough, Abbey helped me build my brand "Called to Inspire," and she brought my ideas on paper to life as a professional brand. Abbey partnered with me in illustrating all my clothing designs and the branding logos, formulating everything I drew and transforming it into digital art. (The cover for this book — yep she did that, too!) Sometimes you have a *kairos* moment[1] and you can either walk in it or let it pass you by. I jumped out of my seat when I saw two gals praying and it led to my business thriving through the power of branding!

That is where the tag line "Wear your uniqueness with confidence" came from in my business. I hope that with the clothing brand, my customers will use my platform to tap into their uniqueness, wearing the styles with confidence in how God created them.

CALLED TO INSPIRE CLOTHING DESIGNS

The designs represent Heaven's colors over Portland.

Subtle Culture

The Subtle Culture design was the first download I received. I often tend to choose abstract and geometric art for my personal decor. From my personal aesthetic style, I created a design that represented my "go to" style while it also portrayed a message of inspiration. I envisioned seven outlined faces that geometrically flowed into one another. The outline of the faces needed a pop of color, so I subtly threw in seven pastel colors on a line of each face. The Subtle Culture name came from the idea of kingdom influence infiltrating each of the seven mountains of culture. Above the faces on the design says the words, "We are all Called to Inspire."

Portland Vibes

The Portland Vibes design is covered with pine trees and words on the side

1 Kairos (Ancient Greek: καιρός) is an Ancient Greek word meaning the right, critical, or opportune moment. https://religionandcivilsociety.com/bible/frequent-question-what-is-a-kairos-moment-in-the-bible.html

that says, "Created to Create. Be bolder than What's Comfortable." I specifically designed Portland Vibes to prophesy over the creatives and believe that the brand would be exposed to them, and that the creative culture would wear this piece of art and receive this declaration. Once I finished the design, I gave it to a friend who represented this kind of culture. She even looked like Portland — with the fringe bangs, tattoos on every inch of her body, and handmade vintage jewelry. This friend holds different religious beliefs from me but she is the niche of people who I hope to reach. When I gave my friend the gift, it was a beautiful exchange as I saw her light up as she laid eyes on the t-shirt. It was as if the gift touched her spirit and the core of who she was without her even fully realizing what she just experienced. I used that special moment as an opportunity to share the gospel and speak truth one-on-one with my friend.

Influence

The Influence design is probably the most well-known one. I cannot tell you the number of people who sent me random texts and pictures of a rainbow saying that they saw a similar rainbow in various boutiques that looked like my brand rainbow. I used pastel colors and included a doorway in the center of the rainbow to make it look distinct from other rainbows.

When the "Influence" design was first launched, a well-known real-estate agent in the community, who I had never met, discovered my t-shirt. She sent me a message sharing that she loved rainbows and ended up buying the shirt and promoting it on her social media. If you look carefully on this design, you will see words at the top of the rainbow, "He has called you by name." The gal who bought the shirt made it clear on her social media that she was involved in new age practices but was attracted to this shirt. I prayed over the clothing line that whoever wears the clothes will encounter the powerful love of Jesus, and receive physical and emotional healing.

My intention in this design is to rightly place the rainbow back to its original design and to proclaim the promises of God. A friend of mine who represented my shirt with the rainbow on it shared that her friend who identified as part of the LGBTQ+ community complimented the shirt and was drawn to the words on the side. My goal in my clothing line is to reach those who won't ever step into a church, and to draw in creative individuals, even though they might not know their creator. As they put on the clothes, they will encounter the living God who placed dreams, color, and creativity inside of them.

Prophetic culture

I received the blueprints of Prophetic Culture in the middle of a revival intercession meeting. One of the leaders of the church called out the creatives and artists in the congregation and declared that those who it resonated with would rise up and tap into their creativity. I perked up when she said it, and immediately stood up. I began picturing mountains, arrows, crowns, and strategies of heaven pouring out onto artists and manifesting on earth on a canvas. I quickly wrote down what I saw on the notes on my phone. The following week, I contacted Abbey to start working on the design project. I combined several components from other designs on this one with a crown that represents kingdom, coffee that points to creativity, arrows to show acceleration, an art palette to show the colors of assignments being released throughout the earth and prophetic words that come to fruition, and the faces from the "Subtle Culture" design to represent the people who are called. I added bright and intense colors such as mustard yellow, teal, hot pinks, and a royal purple.

When I walk into coffee shops, I often get compliments on this particular design, and it surprises people when I share that I made it. I'm not sure why it's usually baristas who compliment the shirt but somehow it speaks to them. Probably because it has coffee beans and rainbows on it.

LIFE COACHING COMPONENT

My workplace experiences guided me to where I am today in my career. I look back at my past workplaces and skills and noticed that every experience — the good, the bad, and the ugly prepared me for the future! The insecurities I may have carried at one point turned into confidence. After my travels to Europe and my decision to stay in Portland long term, it was time to look for a "big girl" job. I knew that I loved to be creative on social media and write. I took a couple of social media marketing classes in college and casually created content for other people free of charge. After applying to at least a dozen companies, I received a follow-up call one day as I was napping. I answered the phone a bit tired and angry but somehow, I still got the job.

Truthfully, I was not qualified, but it was probably one of the best career experiences I gleaned from. I worked as a social media marketer for a high-end medical spa. The company's atmosphere was controlling and I always felt like someone was looking over my shoulder. My two bosses were a husband and a wife team who were both perfectionists and micromanagers. My "Enneagram seven" personality liked flow, freedom, and creativity, but working under this company made it hard to be myself at times. Even though I had to work through a burden of "imposter syndrome" poking at me 24/7, I received many benefits from this company: free red-light therapy, facials, micro-needling, other procedures, and discounts on makeup and products. My skin glowed the entire year I worked there. I looked like a true professional with my fancy lab coat on, but felt so insecure in my skills. My boss continued to encourage me to take classes to grow in the constantly changing social media realm. I am grateful that I took those classes, but doing so continued to remind me that I was not equipped or qualified for the job. Despite that, the favor of the Lord still covered me.

This job equipped and positioned me for where I am today. Although I never felt like myself while working there, that kind of pressure benefitted me in the end as it transformed me into someone who was intentional about becoming excellent in my profession, disciplined me to learn to make fewer errors, and helped me grow in organization skills and communication, giving me a stronger eye for detail. The insecurity I once felt turned into confidence, strength, and an even better career! After looking back, I noticed that the pressure created a deeper level of authority as I pressed on.

The fruit of pushing through in that company later led to getting involved in social media freelance work where businesses hire me to create content on social media. I have experienced freedom now working on my own. It was important to learn the skills I did, because God set me up for success because He knew where He was leading me. What God has *for* you, He often prepares *in* you beforehand.

I started my master's degree in May 2020 while still working full-time at the medical spa. I knew eventually I would transition from my current job to full time business down the road. On my birthday, October 8th, that same year, one of the estheticians named Lindsay gave me a birthday facial. I knew she pursued Jesus with all her heart, and I noticed her gift of hearing God's heart for people through encouragement, dreams, and prophetic words, as she shared about her life with me during and between appointments.

While she gave me that facial, she shared a dream she had of me the night before. In the dream, she pictured me leaving the spa and witnessed me running after my dreams. My boss and Lindsey both were also in the dream. Lindsay told my boss in the dream, "I want to do what she is doing!" What a special birthday present — getting a confirming word. At that point, the only people who knew I was seeking a new direction on the job front were my parents. I knew God was speaking through her about my future dreams of pursuing my life coaching business! The following month, I lowered my job hours from forty to thirty while attending my second semester. Both of my bosses supported my decision. At the end of December of 2020, I left the medical spa.

God gave me a wonderful coaching supervisor during school who supported me in my dreams and helped me navigate the coaching realm, giving me the confidence I needed. In January 2021, I hosted a business launch expressing to the world that I decided to run after my life coaching dreams.

Life coaching soon became a crucial piece to my business. A year after launching Called to Inspire, I added life coaching services in January 2021. Encouraging and helping people find what they are born to do has always been a part of my personality and mission. Ever since a young age, I could envision parts of someone's destiny over those I encountered, even if they were not walking in it or didn't believe it themselves. However, at the time, I did not know this was the gift of discernment and prophecy. I would even see words on people's foreheads and share with them the words I saw.

I always thought I would be involved in some sort of ministry. However, I did not see myself in the business mountain until just a couple of years ago. Surprisingly, Called to Inspire is one of the ways I minister. In my early education as a freshman, I pursued psychology and counseling for about a month, but changed my major to communications and journalism and finished my bachelor's degree in 2019. It was on my heart to do some sort of counseling, as it runs in my family — my mom is a marriage and family therapist and professor. After finishing my bachelor's degree, I was not interested in pursuing any more education. However, at the beginning of 2020, the word *life coach* continued to pop up and individuals would sporadically approach me with this word *life coach*. Fast forward to March 2020. After doing some research, I decided to pursue my master's degree in human services with a concentration in life coaching at Regent University.

When I first made the decision to pursue my masters degree, I did not hear the voice of the Lord. I love to invite God into my decisions, but I heard silence. Because of the silence, I wondered if I had made the right decision. The week I started my online classes, a friend prayed over me and got a word of knowledge and said, "I just see you getting your master's degree and teaching people how to dream." Right then, I knew that God was cheering me on in my decision. That is exactly what I decided to do. Life coaches teach people how to dream! The only people I had shared my decision with was family, so this was God speaking to me that I made the right decision!

Life Coaching is not regulated like counseling, so most life-coaching courses take about six months to become a certified coach. A counseling degree was limiting for the type of services I wanted to offer. Through my master's program, I finished school within a year and a half. Coaching fits my personality, and I also received some incredible counseling techniques and skills from my education. I pursued education and finished my master's in May 2021; but another component to the coaching education that has been very significant to me is the spiritual side, which includes authority, leadership, and influence.

Key #13: Influence is about territory and strategy!

I did not learn the art of authority and influence in a classroom, but through my journey of living in Portland, attending Father's House under Steve's leadership, and serving as an intern. Spiritual influence isn't sharing on social media one's favorite makeup line products and encouraging viewers to purchase them. It's all about territory and strategy! Father's House equipped me and others to walk in authority in our areas of influence, and to bring city transformation while working in the front lines of culture as we position the city and region for revival. I learned the gift of discipling others and boldly proclaiming the gospel through evangelism. The greatest treasure I received in serving under Father's house was learning the strategy of inviting Heaven's culture to invade Portland, in the same territory where the gates of hell had once been entrenched. One of Steve's sermons on the seven mountains inspired me to do the photoshoot I wrote about. The different ways spiritual and practical skills the leadership has taught me while serving them has manifested in my business in a creative way.

Called to Inspire is an outpouring of who I am even down to the feminine style of the colors and the abstract quirky feel of my designs. Much of the way I have created my coaching services and formatted my work is a legacy of Steve's influence and a result of tapping into the fruit of creativity in the city of Portland. I am continuing this legacy through works of art in my clothing designs, through equipping clients under my coaching services, and through hosting Kingdom-inspired events and workshops that train leaders to confidently walk in their God-given assignments. I have learned a lot through counseling classes and coaching techniques, but nothing beats the amount of experience and spiritual training I have received living in the Pacific Northwest that has brought me to where I am today. Called to Inspire is a minimalist and aesthetically pleasing brand, but also a tangible testimony of getting through the other side of being disciplined and rising above the darkness and influencing dark places. I could not teach people how to transform their neighborhoods or influence their workplaces if I had not gone through the process myself.

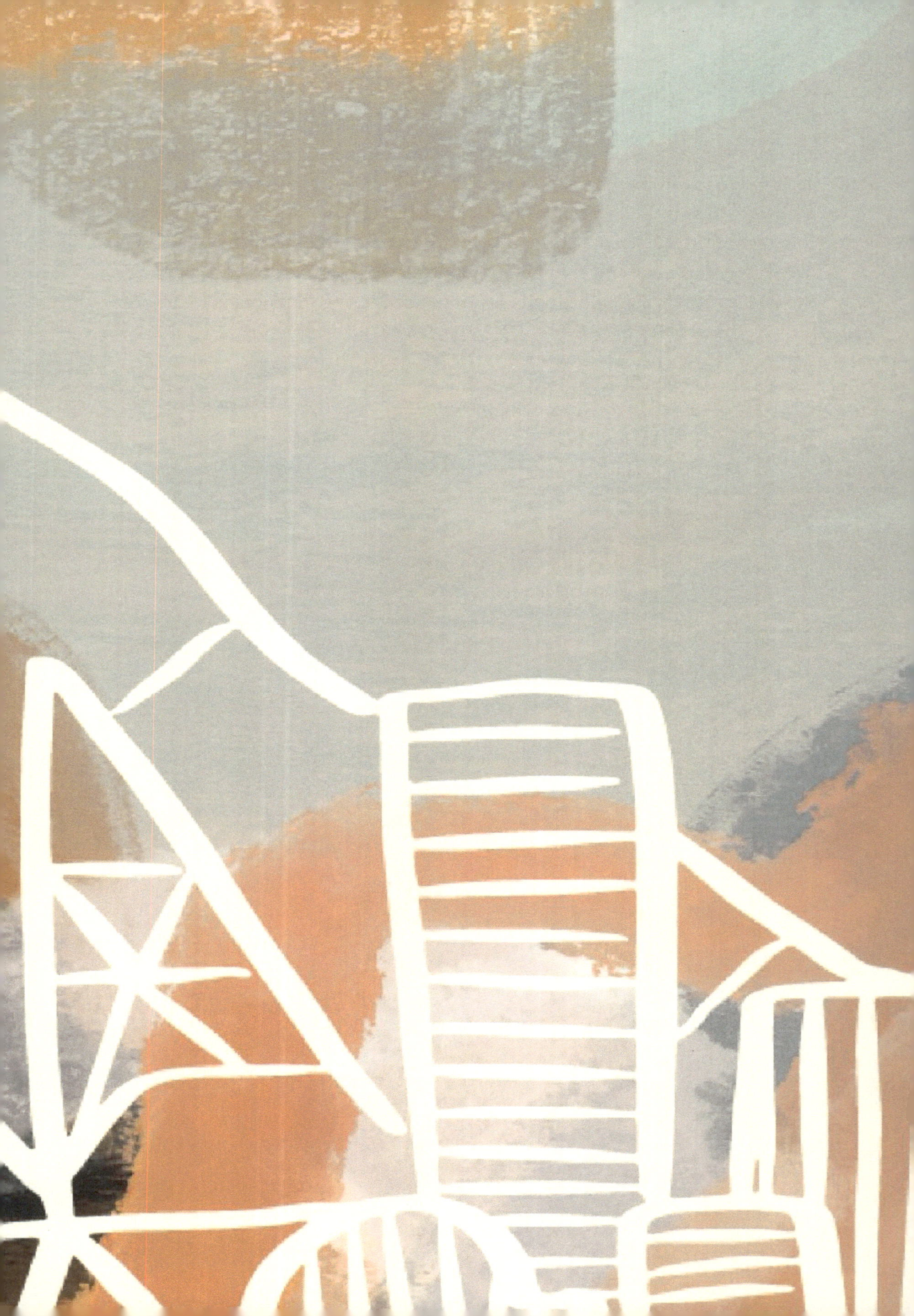

BRIDGING THE GAP

I am an advocate for Portland. After living here for a while now, people assume that I have lived in the city all my life. I kindly tell them that I'm originally from the east coast but greatly appreciate the compliment. I now live across the river in Vancouver, Washington, just about twenty minutes from downtown Portland.

THE DIVISION BETWEEN PORTLAND AND VANCOUVER IS SPIRITUAL:

There is a deeper stronghold behind the tension between Portland and Vancouver, WA which is just across the bridge. A year after living in Portland I moved to Vancouver. Since moving there, I experienced the people in the two cities bashing one another, thinking one is better than the other. I have heard people in Vancouver say out loud, "Portland needs to burn"; "Portland deserves to suffer." Those words are an agreement with a demonic assignment to destroy Portland. Those words carry death and destruction. Through jealousy and arguments, we have given the enemy an easy pathway to start division between the cities. I am here to be a bridge and speak life over both cities. Yes, Vancouver may carry more peace and is a refuge and on Portland's worst days it may look like a war zone but we must hang on to the hope and the destiny over Portland.

It takes unity to make that happen. If you live in Vancouver or in another city that has heard terrible things about Portland in the news, are you going to agree with what you see and hear or will you listen to what heaven has to say over it? Will you agree with heaven and gaze at the colors of Portland that point to the treasure beneath the darkness? Your agreements hold greater power than you know. I guarantee that heaven has better thoughts about Portland than anyone who can see with their natural eyes.

I often hear people say, "You *wear* Portland." These words touch my heart because that's the goal — I *wear* Portland to be in the culture and transform it from the inside out. A friend once told me "I thought you were a liberal because of your clothes!"

If God can redeem buildings, He can redeem cities. For my twenty-fourth birthday, I booked a room at the Society Hotel in the Old town area for a "staycation." The location was where the Father's House team worshipped during the summer while focusing on the streets of Old Town, one of the most run-down parts of Portland. The hotel used to be a flop house where sex trafficking took place and where the shanghai tunnels connected to (see chapter two). Neither I nor the ladies who stayed with me slept much that night, since most of us were feelers and felt the weight of the history of the building and were troubled by the surrounding commotion from outside.

I chose to be an advocate for Portland, no matter what the circumstances look like. At moments, Portland resembles a war zone, but its original design is to be a creative place and hub where the people align with their identities as children of God, and partner with Heaven's blueprints to manifest the culture of Heaven in Portland.

I chose to not agree with words that I have heard: "Let Portland burn." "Portland is just too dark." "Portland has gone too far." "There is no hope for the homeless and the drug issues."

I choose to look at Portland through Heaven's eyes.

Key #14: I have discovered that there is usually breakthrough and destiny underneath all the resistance.

There is a reason why God has, and is, continuing to move and align evangelists, entrepreneurs, creatives, and leaders in the Pacific Northwest. He is preparing and aligning His people together to release something powerful in this region that will impact the whole world.

All eyes were on Portland during the riots: get ready hell: all eyes are going to witness the glory of Jesus in Portland!

Thank you for reading my crazy, radical stories. All these stories have shaped who I am today. Each moment of the process of this dance with the Lord, He went behind and before me, through the laughter, tears, and the pain. The times where my feelings got in the way of the promises, the victory had already been won. God was not surprised by any of the attacks that came my way. I am blessed to have lived through them as they strengthened my spirit, awakened the parts of me that call me higher, and gave me eyes to see that bringing heaven to earth can happen.

Never forsake your experiences. Sometimes you might feel like you are on the front lines of hell and the spiritual warfare may seem strong and intimidating, but He who lives in you is greater than he who lives in the world!

You are called to transform the culture where you live. You are equipped and called. Heavens resources are available. What are you waiting for? What are you going to do now with the tangible resources and knowledge that you cannot unseen after reading this? You were made to bring heaven to earth in everything you put your hands to. You now know the true destiny over Portland. This is what it looks like to take the territory back for the kingdom and uncover heaven's blueprints over the cities.

How are you going to transform the culture where you live? Don't believe what you see in the natural. Look to the colors of Heaven that are revealed to those who seek.

Let's look back at the questions from the first chapter and see if you have gathered a new perspective or received any new revelation.

1. How does God speak to you? Are you open to hearing him in multiple ways?
2. How do you battle spiritual warfare when you are feeling attacked emotionally or physically? How do you wear your armor? (Talked about in Ephesians 6)
3. What Mountain(s) of influence has God called you to? Media, Business/Economy, Arts + entertainment, Family, Religion, Government, and Education.
4. Do you partner with the Holy Spirit to bring His presence, love, and glory into your city, neighborhood, house, or workplace? What does that look like for you to invite the presence of God into these spaces?
5. Do you have a grounded spiritual community who supports you, even corrects you at times, but most importantly cover you in prayer when you need it most?
6. Do you believe you are creative and if so, what does it look like to invite the Holy Spirit into that creative space? Keep these questions in the forefront of your mind as we journey through *The Colors of Portland* together.

LIST OF ALL THE KEYS:

ADDITIONAL RESOURCES ON CITY TRANSFORMATION

Enlow, Johnny. *The Seven Mountain Mantle: Receiving the Joseph Anointing to Reform Nations.* Lake Mary: FL: Creation House, 2009.

——. *RISE: A Reformer's Handbook for the Seven Mountains.* 7 Mountain Publishing, 2018.

Mattera, Joseph. *Kingdom Awakening: A Blueprint for Personal and Cultural Transformation.* Shippensburg, PA: Destiny Image Publishers, 2010.

School of City Transformation. https://www.schoolofcitytransformation.org/

called to inspire

The mission of *called to inspire* is to create a culture and a space to equip and advance those to walk in authority on the front lines of culture. Our services offer kingdom strategies and principles to bring heaven to earth.

called to inspire services and products encompass:

- Social Media Marketing + Branding Services
- Life and Leadership Coaching: Individual 1 on 1 sessions and in corporate spaces.
- PNW Events + Educational Workshops
- Merch: Clothing designs

ABOUT THE AUTHOR

Victoria Kent, author of *The Colors of Portland,* calls herself a creative, and is a life and leadership coach, as well as an entrepreneur. She believes she is called to inspire, empower, and engage those seeking to develop in their areas of influence and purpose. As Victoria moved to the west coast in 2018, her heart has grown to see kingdom leaders walking in confidence and authority, bringing heavenly strategies and blueprints to every mountain of influence. Victoria loves to curate spaces by collaborating with other leaders as she hosts educational events and workshops. Outside of business endeavors, you will most likely find Victoria in a local coffee shop drinking a lavender latte or walking around downtown Portland, Oregon.

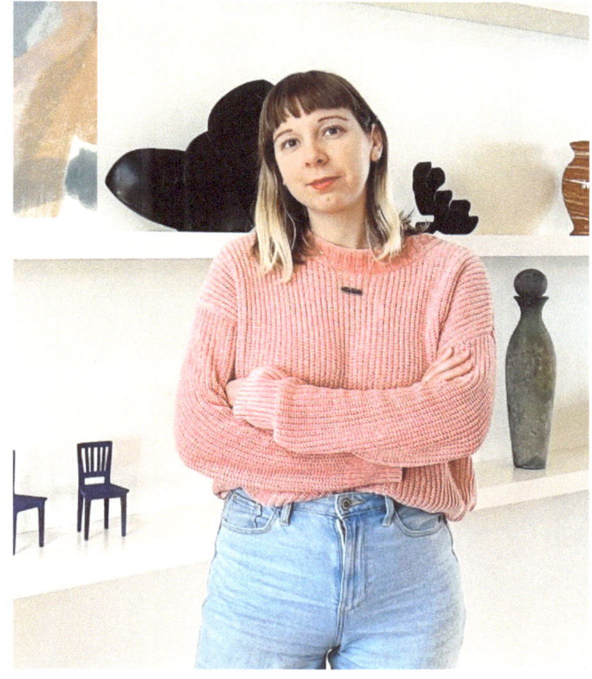

CPSIA information can be obtained
at www.ICGtesting.com
Printed in the USA
BVHW022031170422
634561BV00001B/3